NINE LIVES

A Story of Survival and Hope: Overcoming
Obstacles, Labels and Beating the Odds

Paul Nemiroff, PhD, MD, FACS
with Brian Solon

NINE LIVES

A Story of Survival and Hope: Overcoming
Obstacles, Labels and Beating the Odds

Dr. Paul Nemiroff
with Brian Solon

First Edition

Published by King Michaels, LLC
c/o John Waskom
2033 Main Street—Suite 600
Sarasota, Florida 34237

Front cover photo: Becky Thurner Braddock

ISBN-10: 0692289763
ISBN-13: 978-0692289761

GENERAL DISCLAIMER
Information in this book is for educational purposes only. The
author and the publisher assume no liability or responsibility
for any adverse effects or consequences resulting from the
suggestions, preparations, or procedures mentioned in this
book. You must discuss all your medical issues with your
health care professional. If you are currently under a health
professional's care, you should share any major changes in
your health immediately. Because this is a book (and not a
medical consultation), please keep in mind that the information
presented in this book may not apply to your case. In view of
individual medical requirements, new research, and
government regulations, it is the responsibility of you, the
reader, to talk with your health care professional, before
beginning any supplement or treatment program.

Dedicated to Patrice

NINE LIVES

A Story of Survival and Hope: Overcoming
Obstacles, Labels and Beating the Odds

INTRODUCTION

The challenges we face throughout our lives can be perceived as barriers or stepping stones, depending on how you view them. This shapes our vision of our world and ourselves. Overcoming challenges makes us stronger, inspires us to experiment, and ask questions—to get to the heart of the matter.

I wrote this for those who didn't listen when they were told they weren't good enough, smart enough, or strong enough to fulfill their dreams—but who held tightly to the mantra inside them that said, "Go ahead and do it." I hope this book will be an encouragement to all those who have been told they have less time than they had hoped for, but continue to beat the odds. For those whose lives were defined for them, but who refused to fit the mold, and those who were told they couldn't get what they wanted, but pressed forward anyway—I hope this resonates.

This is the story of a father, husband, nationally recognized surgeon, PhD psychologist, firefighter, university professor, jewelry salesman, entrepreneur, award-winning TV Medical Correspondent, inventor, writer, medical director, marathon runner (13 in all including Boston's 100th) and McDonald's® employee (when only 26,000 were sold)—and now one of a **patient.**

It is for those who have experienced paralyzing fear when their doctor said, "We need to talk." It is for all the families to whom I've had to give the worst possible news. It is for those who want to join my quest to explore new ways to treat and beat cancer. I hope this book provides some solace and hope.

Despite the many obstacles I've faced, I feel blessed to have lived this story and have learned to take nothing for granted—aspiring to live each day with gratitude and humility (still a work in progress) and treasure both the challenges and the rewards. I am one of the luckiest men alive.

Paul Nemiroff, PhD, MD, FACS

Palm Springs, California

2014

1

THE PHONE CALL

I'd just finished giving a lecture to a group of middle school kids about the "evils" of cigarette smoking and was feeling pretty good about myself—a head and neck-cancer surgeon doing his best to convince a bunch of wonderful 8th graders that lung, throat, and oral cancer were killers you could avoid, just by making smart decisions. It was the *Great American Smoke-Out Day* around the country, devoted to educating young people about the perils of tobacco. The date was November 18th, 1999.

Windows down, I sped down the highway on a warm Alabama day with the scent of fall in the air as I listened to a classic Elvis tune blasting from the speakers of my old BMW. I took the exit off Route 72 and worked my way towards my neighborhood.

I had just turned 50 and was reeling and in shock from a recent divorce, which resulted in my children being pulled away to another state—however I was flying to see them every other weekend, much to my physical and emotional exhaustion. I had a booming medical practice and was thinking about running

1

another marathon. But I had to admit I wasn't feeling 100% lately—if it wasn't night sweats or fevers, it was some upper respiratory nonsense. Recently I had been hospitalized with something called "pneumococcal pneumonia," a nasty number that could very well have killed me. I chalked it up to age and overwork. I thought, "You get over it and move on. It happens to everyone."

As I was turning my car into the Edgewater Complex, with thoughts of an early evening run, my car phone rang. The voice on the other end was Dr. Richard Gualtieri—friend, physician, and all around good human being. It was 3:31 p.m. on November 18th, 1999, and the way I looked at the world and my life was about to change forever.

"Hey Rich, What's up?" Rich wasn't in the mood for small talk, and his tone was grave. "Where are you?" he asked. "I'm in the car, heading home."

"Pull over for a second, Paul. We need to talk," Gualtieri said.

There are moments in our lives that forever change us—and this was one of them. I pulled over next to the parkway and turned off the music. As Rich began to speak, my mind went numb. I closed my eyes and my mind momentarily faded to black as I flashed back to a recent life-and-death situation in the operating room...

"We're losing him—Doctor Nemiroff, we're losing him—I can't get an airway!" screamed the anesthesiologist. "I can't get an airway—can't see his vocal cords." In a moment, which seemed to pass in slow motion, the man on the operating room table lost all color. His pulse dropped to

virtually nothing and his oxygen saturation plunged precipitously. Alarms in the operating room were going off everywhere in full force.

Instinctively, I started to crack out orders: "15 blade, Hemostat, Mets, Spreader, Number 8 shiley"—all tools used in performing a tracheostomy, or cutting an airway into a person's throat. In about 60 seconds, in what was essentially a bloodless field, I managed to adroitly and quickly do a "trach," as we call it, and bring the patient back from near death.

After traching this young man, I then had the awesome responsibility of telling his family what had just happened, realizing I still had a 10-hour surgery ahead of me to cure this man of his cancer. Breaking scrub, pulling off mask and gown, I left the O.R. and splashed cold water on my face. I took a deep breath and told them to "prep" the patient for the remainder of the surgery, as I wanted to speak with the family before we started the main procedure. I always strived to be honest and transparent with patients and their families, and wanted them know as soon as possible, directly from me, what was happening in the O.R.

I told the family that there was some initial "excitement" and that we had to perform an emergency trach on him first. I explained that he was doing fine now, and we were going to proceed with his extensive cancer surgical procedure. I also told the wife and family I would give them updates throughout the day from the operating room. My presence seemed to calm some of their apprehension and I could see them visibly relax as their shoulders came down and they all took a deep breath. The patient ultimately did fine—he had an "uneventful" recovery and was in fact cured of his cancer.

Sometimes at the end of a long arduous case, after a 12-15 hour day, I would jokingly pull off my surgical gown and gloves and say in a sardonic way: "Another day of saving lives—every day's a party." The O.R. crew would beg me to come up with another line, but they had heard it for years. Life and death are a part of a surgeon's existence.

Suddenly I snapped out of my flashback, back to Rich's voice. He was delivering news that left me absolutely breathless. Something ominous had shown up on my bone marrow report and he wanted to see me first thing the next morning in his office.

A couple of weeks earlier, on November 5th, I'd had a bone marrow biopsy based on the fact that I was having numerous infections, and a relatively low white blood cell count. I hadn't thought too much about it—however, for perhaps a year or so, I had been getting a lot of infections—and had quietly been getting my blood cell counts measured.

I noted that my white counts, the ones that fight infection, were relatively low. Previous insurance physicals usually had mine around 8500, now they were frequently down to 3000-3500. It seemed to occur about every 4-6 weeks—and I figured it must be something called "cyclic neutropenia," which refers to a benign condition where your white cell numbers can cycle up and down. Somewhat naïvely, I had told my oncologist friend Rich, why not just give me a shot of Neupogen®—a drug they give people undergoing chemotherapy to boost their white blood cell production. I was just tired of being sick. Rich, appropriately, was reluctant to do that, being the good doc that he is, and insisted on doing a bone marrow biopsy to make a proper diagnosis.

"It's probably nothing," he said, "but let's just do a routine bone marrow biopsy."

"Those are no fun," I said. "I've done them on patients myself." He reassured me, "Don't worry about it." On November 5th, they booked me for the procedure under a "phony name," since I didn't want anybody thinking I was sick or anything. Besides, it was just a "routine bone marrow." I didn't think that much of it. I remember laughing as I was being wheeled into the procedure room for the test, because I wasn't the one "scrubbed," and was in one of those patient gowns— with the back open—causing one to feel and look "very exposed."

The procedure went well—no problems—and that was about it. They said they would call me with the results. I didn't think about it much until that fateful phone call on November 18th. When the phone rings and you hear a solemn, foreboding tone of your personal physician saying, "We need to talk"—it stops you in your tracks.

Rich suspected I had a malignant blood disorder called Myelodysplastic Syndrome, or "MDS." MDS consists of many different types and forms—and all can be deadly. At one time, they were called "smoldering leukemia" or "pre-leukemia," but today it is considered as a form of blood cancer, with no real cure, except the possibility of a bone marrow transplant in some very limited cases.

MDS has many symptoms and signs, one of which is not being able to properly fight infections. Thus, being exposed to people with wound infections or respiratory infections, or for that matter any kind of infection, would put my life in peril. At that moment, I began to realize that not only did I have a life-threatening illness, but also that I would be putting myself in harm's way by practicing my very profession. I was going to potentially lose my life—and in the process also *lose my identity as a surgeon.*

I asked Rich to repeat the diagnosis several times. My knowledge of MDS, at that time, was very limited, so when I asked him how serious it was, he said, "I've never really told anybody the details over the phone—I'll tell you tomorrow." I responded, "You just told me how serious it is. How long?" He was quiet for a second then said, "Let's talk tomorrow."

Standing on the deck of my home that evening after that dire phone call of November 18th, 1999, I remember looking at the gorgeous sunset. My first thought was that I wouldn't see my two little daughters grow up. As I spiraled into this thought pattern, I began to think about other things I might miss, like a first date for my daughters, or their graduating from high school, or simply not being able to spend time with them. It hit me that I'd better start to wake up and learn to "smell the coffee."

In my decades of practice, I had never cancelled a clinic full of patients. However, that night I called my wonderful business manager Brenda and asked her to reschedule all my appointments with other doctors in my practice. I felt incredibly selfish for doing this, but I knew the next morning I would be immersed in discussions with my oncologist friend about next steps. **The doctor had become the patient.**

2

BORN IN EAST LA

clad in sombrero at age 10 months

It seemed as if I spent half my early childhood recovering from colds and flus on the big brown couch, or from my day bed in my family's tiny home in Montebello, East Los Angeles. I have no idea why I was such a sickly child.

My father came from hardy Russian stock. He would wake up every morning at 2 a.m. and drive his truck downtown to buy produce from the wholesalers, which he would then sell to the markets and restaurants throughout the city. When he was only four years old, he became an orphan. He and his seven older brothers and sisters—there were 12 originally—fled Russia after violent pogroms targeting Jews, and immigrated to the United States. He would later live through the horrors of Normandy, as an American soldier, later returning to Chicago where he had originally met my mother, who was also of Ukrainian / Russian stock.

I still remember my father's advice to me and my older brother, Art: "If you work hard, you can have anything you want." His other bit of wisdom, I suspect from a Russian proverb, was: "The rougher the road, the smoother the ride." I'm sure it lost something in translation, but it has to do with working hard. He was a model of the American work ethic, and for that I'm thankful.

But there I was, this sickly child growing up in the 1950s, missing more school days than any of my classmates, to the point where I was unable to keep up. We never learned exactly what was wrong with me. We went to several different doctors, but the diagnosis was never conclusive. Hypotheses ranged from allergies to something called "leukemia"—but the tests always came back with more questions than answers.

To comfort myself though the feelings of loneliness and frustration, I spent countless hours watching cartoons from my bed. My closest companion was a guy named "Skipper Frank" who came on during the breaks between shows and introduced the next set of cartoons. He was a middle-aged man on a local TV station touting a captain's hat and gripping a ship's helm. Day after day I'd turn on the TV and there he'd be, announcing cartoons with his booming voice and big smile. It was comforting to see his face—I suppose with all of the unknowns in my life, I looked to him to make things better.

The Label

When I was eight, we moved to a slightly nicer neighborhood in North Hollywood. The third grade teacher there was a cruel woman. If I asked too many questions, she would sit me in the corner, place a pointy "dunce cap" on my head, and seal my mouth with duct tape—which she would later rip off, taking some skin along with it. Through my tearing eyes I could see the taunting looks from my classmates. This abuse continued until my mother saw my bleeding face one day and complained to the principal. The public humiliation ceased, but the ridicule from my fellow students did not.

The "dumb kid" image became a permanent brand in the sixth grade when my mother received a call from the school informing her that a standardized test revealed that I was a "slow" child. It was unlikely, she was told, that I would ever make it to college, if I even managed to make it through high school. They commented that I would only be able to do "manual" labor. I guess the counselor, in one way, was right—since as a surgeon I used my hands every day.

"You're not slow," my mother reassured me. "You're not slow at all, you just have to learn to read better." My mother believed in me, encouraged me, and always found a few extra dollars for a book if I needed it or wanted it, once I learned how to read. When I had doubts about how others perceived me, she would say, "What's not to like?" Children of any age, race, faith or background all need some "watering" to grow to their full potential. Many times, a simple gesture, compliment, or legitimate praise from a parent or adult can be life-changing.

My frustration of not being able to read continued—the words just didn't make sense to me. I wasn't dyslexic—there was a new system taught in schools called "sight reading," which replaced phonetic based reading—and since I'd missed a lot of school on account of being sick, it just didn't register. Early struggles with reading would later develop into a phobia for standardized testing in my educational life—all the way until medical school.

As for my recurring infections, those disappeared when I started receiving regular immune-boosting gamma globulin shots. I used to dread those injections—that big needle going into my little arm or rear end. But the doctor was a kind man, and the shots did their job. I stopped being sick and missing classes. I knew then my life's calling was to become a doctor. There were no other doctors in my extended family, let alone anyone who had a college degree, so this aspiration seemed far-fetched. Our social class was much more modest.

Get Your Kicks

Money was always tight and we seldom traveled anywhere. One exception was when the four of us drove cross-country from LA to Chicago to visit relatives in an old car without AC during the height of summer. It was a long horrible trip in a crowded car. One thing I remember was that this was the year Marilyn Monroe died. I was wondering what was all the fuss—later I realized.

On the way to Chicago along the famed Route 66, my Dad left his wallet somewhere in New Mexico. We would have to wait in Amarillo, Texas for a few days until the clerk (who had first extracted 50 dollars) sent it along. Approaching Texas, I tortured everyone in the car, claiming I knew how people talked there. In my best, most exaggerated Texas accent that I'd gleaned from watching TV, I would repeatedly bellow, *"We're gonna be deeeeeeep in the heart—of Texas."* Finally my brother was ready to strangle me, and I held him off saying, "You just wait 'til we get there, and you'll see."

Upon arriving in Amarillo, we asked a friendly local where the post office was. He responded, "It's over there, folks. Now you're deeeeep in the heart of Texas!" My Mom and Dad laughed, and I felt sweet vindication.

With the exception of this big vacation, the only other "outings" we enjoyed were a couple trips to the *Date Festival* in Indio, near Palm Springs California—a parade of Native Americans celebrating the date harvest. They would toss a few dates into the sidelines, and I was thrilled to catch a few. Years later, the Palm Springs area would become my refuge, almost a magical healing sort of place.

The Wash

At age 12, I was riding my bike with my friend Glen through "the wash," an aqueduct-like system used for drainage in the San Fernando Valley. In my pocket I was carrying $10—two weeks pay from my paper route job—which I planned to bring to the bank and cash in for rolls of pennies to supplement my coin collection—always looking for that rare gem.

Suddenly, a group of gang members attacked us. Glen managed to get away on his bike, however I wasn't so lucky—now alone to face the four thugs who demanded my money.

"Come on," the leader ordered, "hand it over."

Hoping they would let me go, I gave him my $10 bill, but it wasn't enough.

"Hold him down," the leader said with a twisted grin. "It's time for some target practice."

He then pulled out his slingshot and stepped back ten paces while the others held me down and placed a rock on top of my head. I pleaded with them to let me go, but it was useless. The leader loaded his slingshot, took aim at the target rock on top of my head—and missed, hitting me with great force square in my right eye. The pain was excruciating. When I fell to the ground screaming that I couldn't see, the four kids took off in a hurry.

Somehow I managed to make it home. No one was there—my parents had left for the evening and my brother Art was out on a date. Fortunately, I had enough sense to put ice on my face. When Art got home, he called my parents and they rushed me to the emergency room, where I overheard the doctors saying that I had about a 50/50 chance of losing the vision in my eye.

Through the grace of God, my vision slowly returned. After weeks of wearing a patch, I was able to see again and go out and play with the rest of the kids. However, during the testing of my vision, the doctors discovered that I was colorblind. To really understand what this means, search online for a picture of an "Ishihara color plate." While this meant nothing to me at the time, this condition would put an end to another dream I had— attending the Air Force Academy and eventually becoming an astronaut—as I would later learn when I took flying lessons that I couldn't distinguish between the red and green landing lights. Color blindness also almost kept me from becoming a surgeon.

Enter Judo

After my run-in with the thugs, I took a bike ride with my friend Peter from the San Fernando Valley to Disneyland—an 80-mile round trip, using side streets. As I rode on my red ten-speed used Schwinn bike, I noticed a martial arts studio, or "dojo." It was getting dark, and Peter needed to go home, but I was intrigued and wanted to explore.

The teacher, or Sensei, welcomed me in. It was a brand new school, and for a long time I was his only student. With all the personalized attention, I became quite good. Day after day I would go to this dojo, practicing my "katas" and learning to take "falls," as well as learning the art, science, and spirit of the discipline.

Learning judo was a life-changing experience, both physically and mentally. I advanced to first-degree brown belt (ik-kyu), which built my confidence. Years later I would win a judo tournament in college that (combined with good grades) gained me a life-saving scholarship, which allowed me to continue my education. Later I would visit and take lessons at a Chuck Norris studio.

The Light Switch

The turning point in my education came when I took the Evelyn Wood speed-reading course. It was like somebody flipped a light switch on inside me. Suddenly I developed an insatiable appetite for books—science books in particular. Money was always tight, but my mother was always there to buy me a book. Maybe it was because I had spent so much time in doctors' offices, unpleasant as that was, but medicine became an early fascination.

One of my first books was Bernard Glemser's classic illustrated children's book *All About the Human Body*. I became fascinated with anatomy. My mother never tired of telling everyone how I woke her up from a nap one afternoon to show her the still-beating heart I had dissected out of a large bullfrog—after anesthetizing it, of course—and per the biology class instructions. She was convinced at that point that her smiling son was destined to become a surgeon, though the road to medicine would be anything but a direct one for me. My first diversion was in keeping with the national obsession of the day—*The Race For Space*.

Rocket Boy

It started one afternoon when my cousin, a scientist at Space Technology Laboratories (later to become TRW), took my brother and me on a tour of the facility. There in front of us were the original backup satellites used by NASA. It many cases, they were no bigger than the size of a basketball, with what appeared to be spikes sticking out. Like so many kids my age, I dreamed of becoming an astronaut. I began reading everything I could about rocket science. Before long I was building and launching my own rockets.

One of the books I read explained how zinc and sulfur could be combined to make a "fairly stable" rocket fuel. Without fully understanding the purpose of my mission, my mother drove me to the local hardware store where I was able to buy canisters of powdered zinc. A local nursery became a source of sulfur, which was used as fertilizer at the time.

Fortunately I had the good sense to use only wooden tools— wooden bowls and spatulas "borrowed" from my mother's kitchen—to avoid creating any sparks in the preparation of my rocket fuel. I was able to obtain metal tubing for my rocket fuselages from various junkyards. A local machinist was kind enough to help me manufacture my rocket nozzles.

In all, I must have launched a dozen rockets. The Granddaddy was one I named *Venture One*. The design came from a rocket manual written at Fort Sill, Oklahoma, home of the Field Artillery School—where, many years later, I would spend some of my time in the Army. *Venture One* stood four feet tall. In theory, it could reach close to a mile and a half in altitude, with the possibility of breaking the sound barrier.

After months of work, my cousin Steve drove me out to the desert near Edwards Air Force base where the two of us set up to launch *Venture One*. Unfortunately, things didn't go exactly as planned. The fins I had bolted onto the rocket to give it stability ripped off during the powerful launch, and the rocket, now a missile, spun out of control, with cousin Steve and I running for our lives, taking cover under his car. There we waited anxiously for what we hoped would be *Venture One's* soft return to earth.

The mechanism I had designed for the rocket's parachute was based on a mercury switch. Once the rocket reached its peak altitude and turned earthward, the liquid mercury inside would tip over, completing an electrical connection. This would light an old-fashioned hot flashbulb, which in turn would ignite a gunpowder fuse that would burn through a rubber band holding down a spring. Once the spring was released, the nose cone of the rocket would open, releasing the parachute. The mechanism worked—sort of. Unfortunately, all I had to show for my work was a mangled piece of metal plummeting to earth.

Miami

Undaunted, I continued my rocketry experiments—since our high school science and biology class required "projects." I sent up fertilized chicken eggs, which I managed to retrieve undamaged. I then watched to see how they would develop. I also sent up mice. I developed a wooden maze to see how quickly the mice could find the cheese before and after being launched into "space." A turtle with "Miami" painted on his underbelly made it through several space flights. At one point I considered obtaining a spider monkey and teaching him how to push a button that would deploy the parachute. Fortunately for the monkey, I did not have the money to conduct this experiment.

Aerial photography was next. I had heard that sulfuric acid, when mixed with zinc, releases hydrogen gas. I got the acid from a neighbor who used it to clean his swimming pool. Wearing rubber gloves I had again "borrowed" from my mother's kitchen and a swimming mask to protect my eyes—there was no telling which way this one could go—I dropped the zinc into a bottle filled with the acid. I then quickly covered the top of the bottle with a balloon, which immediately inflated with the hydrogen gas, and launched the balloon into the air—attached to a string.

I equipped the balloon with an old-fashioned Kodak® camera, which I had jury-rigged with a time-delay switch using Silly Putty® (a pliable clay-like substance), a straw, and a rubber band. The idea was for the straw to hold the camera shutter lever in the "up" position while the rubber band was pulling it down. The Silly Putty would slow the speed at which the lever would pull downwards, giving my balloon time to gain altitude for the aerial photos. I didn't get much in the way of photos, but no harm was done, which is more than I can say for my foray into rocket thrust.

The Rocket Sled

For this experiment, I had built a rocket sled using an old-fashioned roller skate and a miniature railroad track. The rocket skate was then tethered to a fish scale (covered in wax from a candle), which I had attached to the outside garage wall. If everything went as planned, I would be able to determine how many pounds of thrust a particular rocket was delivering as it pulled at the fish scale, and would leave a mark on the wax surface of how many pounds of thrust had occurred. Unfortunately, the rocket I had devised for this particular experiment had too much thrust and it ripped the fish scale out of the wall and took off, blowing a hole into the back of our garage and leaving me with a lot of explaining to do.

My rocketry experiments continued, but the idea of one day becoming a physician never left my mind. I pondered the links between life in space and medicine. How would the astronauts adapt to weightlessness? How would they handle the G-forces at lift off? How would it affect the human body? Years later, in Huntsville, Alabama (the birthplace of America's space program), I would consult with NASA on the use of the hyperbaric oxygen chamber on the space station, in the same way it is used as a decompression chamber for divers returning from the depths of the ocean.

Seeing Things Differently

I had many odd jobs and saved enough money to buy about 10 hours of flying lessons at Van Nuys airport. One night when we were getting ready to land, the instructor was telling me to follow some colored light patterns on our approach to the runway. When we were at 1500 feet, I asked the instructor "Which colored lights should I follow? You mean the green lights?" She said, "No, they're red."

I would soon take an eye exam for flying that reinforced something I already knew – that I was severely colorblind (or as they say today, "color-deficient"...*please, I'm not that "P.C."*). The doctor doing the test told me "Not only can you never fly at night, you can forget about being a fighter pilot. You're severely color blind." At the time, in the event that your radio went out, they would "bring you in" with color-coded lights: a green for go ahead, a red means continue to circle. I, however, couldn't tell the difference half the time. Color blindness, over the course of my life, would turn out to be a mixed blessing.

On the Run

Making the cross-country team in high school was a big accomplishment. My brother Art had been a star 100-yard dash participant in high school, so they had great hopes when I came along. However I didn't inherit my brother's "fast twitch fibers," as they're called. This meant he could run very fast for short distances. Unlike my brother, I had endurance, but I was still slow and mediocre at best. I remember Coach "Beer Belly Johnson," a purported bronze medalist in an Olympic track event, saying to me, "Neeee-mir-off, you're so slow we are going to need a calendar to follow your pace, rather than a stopwatch." He nicknamed me "The Calendar Boy." I did "letter" in cross-country, in spite of those incredibly "encouraging" words.

Years later I went on to run 13 marathons, including the running of the 100th Boston Marathon. I was never competitive, just a finisher. It was probably some of that discipline from my early days of Judo and cross-country that pushed me to finish those marathons and fight through exhaustion. Having this type of endurance would prove critical in my later days becoming a surgeon, and in my battle with malignant blood cancer, MDS.

Stud Service

Eventually all the lights went on. Still holding onto the dream of one day becoming a doctor, I took all the pre-med sciences classes my high school offered and did quite well. But the labeling of being "slow" still lingered, along with my fear of standardized testing (SATs, for college admissions—GREs for graduate school admission—and MCATs, the required admission test to get into medical school), to the point that I would try to avoid them at all costs.

My self-perception was far different from that of others. When I later attended my 20-year high school reunion, I spoke with alumni and was surprised to learn that others viewed me as a really smart kid. At the time, however, I didn't know it. I was still dealing with the labeling stuff of being "slow." During high school, I'd been active on the steering committee, cross-country, and involved in student service. However, in my yearbook it was shortened to "Stud Service"—I could only hope.

PAUL NEMIROFF
X-Country, Str Comm,
Stud Serv.

Grant High School yearbook—1966-67

When I graduated somewhat early from high school, around age 17, I had my choice of universities. As I looked forward towards college, I was determined to start off on the right foot and succeed. Little did I know that my academic career had barely yet begun—and I would be in school for another 18 years.

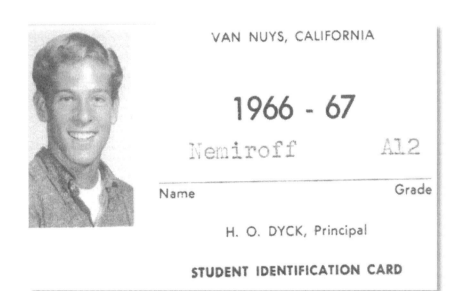

VAN NUYS, CALIFORNIA

1966 - 67

Nemiroff   A12

Name   Grade

H. O. DYCK, Principal

STUDENT IDENTIFICATION CARD

Student ID card featuring—"H.O. DYCK, Principal"

You can imagine how high school kids had fun with that

3

LOST AT SEA

I wanted to get away from the Los Angeles area for college. Ultimately, I chose the University of California at Santa Barbara, which was known for having a good marine biology department, and I figured I could get a good pre-med education there. Plus, it was right on the beach, and I managed to slip in without taking the SATs.

Money was always a problem. My parents could barely scrape together a small portion of the first year tuition, so I was always working part-time jobs to survive, and applied for one of many student loans that would take me years and years to eventually pay off.

The first year, I lived in a dorm just off campus. The next year I was invited to pledge a fraternity, Sigma Chi. Many of the guys in the fraternity house were from well-to-do families and heading into medicine, law and other good professional careers. And most were into sports. I wound up winning a judo competition, which (along with a few other accomplishments) led me to being chosen as the "Sig of the Year," which included a scholarship plus room and board for a year—this coupled with various jobs and loans allowed me to stay in college.

On Friday and Saturday nights, while some of my fraternity brothers were partying, I was at the library studying to get the grades I needed to get into medical school. My grades were OK in general, but I was having trouble with organic chemistry, because of my color blindness. When doing experiments, we had to look for color changes in the test tube before proceeding to the next step. So I never knew when to add the next chemical. "What's wrong with you, Nemiroff?" the professor once asked me. "Can't you see what you are doing?" Actually—with respect to colors—no, I couldn't.

A more positive surprise came in a class I was taking on *Conceptions of Intelligence,* in which we were given every battery of standardized IQ tests, as part of our training. Still harboring the notion that I was not all that bright, I was amazed when the results came back. They must have been someone else's, I thought—I'd scored in the 99th percentile.

The professor asked me to repeat a portion of the test in an enclosed cubicle with a camera on me. He wasn't concerned about my having cheated, he insisted—although I felt singled out. He told me he just wanted to see if I could repeat the results—which I did. Again, I scored in the 99th percentile. He had never seen anyone score that high. He later wrote a beautiful letter of recommendation that helped get me into grad school. The surprising result on that portion of my IQ test, however, didn't do anything to allay my fears of standardized admissions tests, which I would continue to try avoiding at all costs as I advanced through my academic years.

After two years at Santa Barbara, I decided to transfer to UCLA to finish my junior and senior years of undergraduate studies. I figured I'd have a better chance of getting into medical school from a "big name" university, where they also had a medical school. Before the school year began, however, even with my Sigma Chi scholarship, I found myself in desperate need of money to get through the remainder of my college years.

Alcan Highway

In high school and during my two years at UC Santa Barbara, I had worked at a variety of low-paying jobs, like McDonald's and Sears, for $1.50 per hour. That wasn't enough now. I'd heard somewhere that college kids could make "big bucks" up in Alaska working on shrimp boats. That sounded good to me. CJ, a friend from Santa Barbara, who had been in a number of Disney movies as a kid and had a wild streak in him, proved the perfect traveling companion as the two of us set out driving north in his old Volvo to claim our pot of gold.

The drive from Santa Barbara to Fairbanks was nearly 4000 miles, including 1300 miles on the famous "Alcan Highway," which at that time still consisted of many dirt roads and huge potholes. When we finally arrived in Fairbanks, we were greeted with laughter by the locals at the idea of these two college kids expecting to find work on shrimp boats without any experience. So shrimping was out.

After pursuing a bunch of dead end leads, we finally went to the Bureau of Land Management (BLM) and Forestry Service in hopes of getting jobs as forest fire fighters, or "smoke jumpers." In the summer of 1969, the fires in Alaska were burning out of control, but we were told that without any experience, our chances of being hired weren't very good. As luck would have it, one of the BLM directors was a "judoka" (judo practitioner) and he noticed on my application that I had won a competition in college. That got CJ and me our first jobs as forest firefighters. The pay was spectacular—$75 a day, versus the ten bucks a day I'd been making at Sears.

Being a firefighter was hard and dangerous work. We were out there 12 hours a day, 7 days a week. We didn't see a day off for three weeks, which was good, because I didn't spend much money and was able to save it all for college and a car. Prior to this time, all I had was an old 250cc motorcycle.

Our days consisted of making "fire roads"—narrow pathways to isolate burning areas of forest. The tool we used to do this was called a Pulaski, which was nothing more than a hoe on one side and an axe on the other, for cutting through the tundra, or grassy matting, until we hit the hard, rock-like "permafrost"—the frozen ground that never thawed out.

We'd be out there for days, sleeping under the cover of the plastic tents we carried along with us. If we uncovered any "hot spots" during the course of our digging, we'd put them out with the Fedcos—50-pound water-bearing backpacks we all carried, which amounted to little more than a big squirt gun. They wouldn't put out a tree that was torching and about to explode, but they worked on "hot spots," which could smolder underground for months, igniting new fires the next season—or that night. They'd just reignite, starting a new fire, like the trick candles you put on a birthday cake. I woke up from a nap one day to find my boots burning on my feet. One poor fellow went off to take a nap one day and was never found. The bears hadn't gotten him, so we assumed he had just burned up.

Amphibian planes and helicopters took us from one "hot spot" to the next, from the Arctic Circle down to the Kenai Peninsula. For days we sustained ourselves on "C-rations."—used in WWII and Vietnam, they were cans with lead all over them, filled with beans etc.—like MREs of today, but not nearly as tasty. You never knew when things could go wrong.

The most frightening experience came when a dozen of us were dropped off to create a backfire in a heavily wooded area somewhere north of Fairbanks. Suddenly the wind shifted and we were surrounded by flames. Overhead we could see the tankers approaching. Then they started dropping the retardant, which emerged from the planes like a mist and then clumped up and hit the ground like baseballs, splattering as they hit.

"Take cover!" someone would cry. "Don't get this stuff on you." I hid behind an old log. I could feel the heat of the fire, with cinders and lit pieces of branch flying in the air. Suddenly a ranger helicopter appeared and started airlifting us out. They could only take two at a time. I remember a guy yelling at me when I almost walked into the rear blade of the helicopter as I boarded. Fortunately we all made it to safety—possibly accounting for one of my nine lives.

It got scary at times. But one thing I'll always remember was the Arctic moon, which appears 20 times larger as you approach the North Pole. I was right near the Arctic Circle, looking up at one of those moons, when Neil Armstrong made his landing on July 20th, 1969. There we were in the middle of nowhere, with the wild caribou and the raging fires, looking up at this enormous moon and a man I could see in my mind, like us, in the middle of another nowhere. It struck me that day how insignificant we all are in the grand scheme of things—a thought that would recur to me with far greater immediacy on another day, later in my life. We're only here "for a moment."

Go Bruins

At the end of that summer I returned to Los Angeles with enough money for my next year at UCLA and promptly paid cash for my first car—a fire-engine red Datsun 1600 two-seat convertible. It was a "rush" to get this kind of sports car, and especially meaningful that I'd paid for it myself.

I began my junior/senior year at UCLA in the fall of 1969 with a full load of pre-med classes, as well as many courses in psychology—from abnormal psychology, to classes in "stuttering," to one on parapsychology—dealing with things like ESP, which has always been a fascination for me. Life seemed to be going along, but every male my age was concerned about Vietnam. If I got into med school, I might be able to get a deferment, but I still didn't think I could get in, since I hadn't taken the MCATs (the required admissions test) and lacked a couple of courses. While in the midst of contemplating what to do once I graduated, the decision was suddenly thrust in my face for me. I won the "lottery"—the draft board lottery, that is.

I was just ready to finish my bachelor's degree at UCLA when a renewed draft lottery came into effect. I was lucky #42 based on my birthday. The Army, depending on the city, was taking everyone with numbers up to about 200 or so in my area, so I knew I was destined to be drafted. I thought I might be able to get into the Army Reserves, but at the time they were full.

Before I graduated, I had to make a decision and eventually, luckily I did get into the Army Reserves. However, shortly after finishing courses at UCLA, the next thing I knew, I received a "welcome letter" from the US Army saying that I was to report for basic training at Fort Campbell Kentucky, home of the famous 101st Airborne Rangers. I'd never seen my Father shed a tear before, until he said goodbye to me at the airport in LA. He had been in Normandy in WWII. I knew this was not a good sign, and that some "serious stuff" potentially lay ahead.

Upon first arriving at Fort Campbell, I was "greeted" by a massive man, one of the drill sergeants screaming at all of us to "Move it, move it!" One of the first stops was for our special "individualized haircuts." As anyone knows who's been in the service, there are NO individualized haircuts.

Fort Campbell, Kentucky, 1970
(me circled in the top right corner)

When the barber asked me which one of the three styles I might want from those offered in a picture on the wall, I said, "Sir, I'd like the one called the *California Cut*." He replied, "No problem." In about 30 seconds, my head was almost completely shaved, just like everyone else's. I made the mistake of commenting that my haircut didn't quite look like the picture on the wall, and for this comment the drill sergeant made me run around the barracks a half a dozen times while screaming self-deprecating remarks about myself.

While there, I became friends with an African-American kid from Detroit. He told me he had learned to make a living shining shoes. He also said, "I'll show you how to do it," and maybe one weekend we could "win a pass" and go off base for a day or so together. After spending hours "spit shining" my boots, which glistened in the sun, he and I did receive a pass. We quickly put on our khaki uniforms, the travel uniform of the day. (Back then there were three types of uniforms—"fatigues," "khakis," and "dress greens.")

We hitchhiked to somewhere north of Nashville and entered a small little restaurant to have lunch. After waiting a half hour to be served in an uncrowded restaurant, my black friend said, "I don't have a good feeling about this place, let's leave." I responded, "No, we're hungry, let me ask the waitress." What a shock when I heard the comment—"As long as you're with this n-----, you're not getting served either."

A few of the local "bubbas" stood up and told us we'd better leave if we "didn't want no trouble." My friend was grabbing me to leave. Here we were in uniform, just a couple of kids wanting a hamburger, Vietnam raging, and it would be okay for him to risk his life serving his country, but he couldn't get served in this little restaurant. And it wasn't that long ago. It was my first big experience with real racial hatred. I didn't get it.

Hot Steel, On Target, On Time

After leaving Fort Campbell, I was assigned to Fort Sill, Oklahoma, known for its 105 and 155 Howitzers (canons). I eventually ended up in "FDC"—Fire Direction Control. In artillery you have the "FO" (Forward Observer), or "Eyes of the Operation," who is supposed to spot the enemy. Then, you have the guys working the actual canons or howitzers, often called "Canon Cockers," or the "Brawn of the Operation."

Lastly, you had the so-called "Brains of the Operation,"—Fire Direction Control guys. The FDC guys were in a bunker trying to figure out what type of charges to use, calculating wind and other meteorological data. Back then, there were about 4 or 5 of us in each FDC unit. We quickly worked using slide rules to calculate the various data so as to accurately give information to the cannon cockers to direct their fire. The motto of the day was "Hot Steel, On Target, On Time."

Around the time of our "graduation" a primitive new computer was introduced called FADAC (Field Artillery Digital Automatic Computer). It was designed to replace all of us, and do it faster and quicker. Just having finished learning all this stuff with slide rules, we found out we were probably obsolete. In a "race against FADAC," the five of us were able to beat the computer some of the time—however one time we miscalculated so badly we nearly had a shell land on top of us.

One fear we all had was that, regardless of our military status, we could be shipped to Vietnam. This was always held over our heads. So it didn't help when one day a particular drill sergeant came yelling at me to get my "head out of my a--."

At night, during the "war game" maneuvers, where "live rounds" were being used, a red flare was launched, which meant STOP and stay where you are. In contrast, a green light meant: "Go ahead." The flare looked green to me and I said, "Let's go."—until the drill sergeant started yelling at me, "You idiot— it's red!" It was yet another color blindness issue—which could potentially claim another one of my nine lives.

Through the Grace of God, as mentioned, I was able to get into the Army Reserves and realized that although I would still have a 6-year obligation, my chances of going to Vietnam dropped considerably, and by this time the number of troops in Vietnam had been markedly reduced. I knew I would have been destroyed over there in one form or another, and I have tremendous respect for the guys who served there. I was one of the lucky ones.

Island Fever

Having completed my bachelor's degree at UCLA, I had a job interview lined up at Edwards Air Force base in California (which was later used for some Space Shuttle landings)—and the same location where, years earlier, I'd launched *Venture One*. The position seemed like a "glorified clerk" to me. I told them I would let them know whether I would accept it in a couple of weeks after I returned from Hawaii, where I was going with a few friends.

After two weeks in Hawaii, I turned down the job at Edwards and decided not to come home, but stay and live in Hawaii a little longer. One of my friends knew of a place very close to the beach in what I considered was a mansion. The house's owner would rent out several rooms to young professionals.

While in Hawaii, part of my Army Reserve time was spent at Scoffield Barracks, full of history from World War II and Pearl Harbor days. You could still see machine gun holes in the barracks left from the Japanese attack on December 7th, 1941. I knew I was lucky to not have to been in a war.

It was a time of searching for me. I didn't have much money and had sold my sports car earlier and wound up buying a motorcycle again (the first one was one I had was while I was at UC Santa Barbara). After a brief job, search—I finally landed a position as a jewelry salesman at Zales Jewelers on Oahu. I had no experience, but quickly learned all about diamonds and jewelry.

I worked 12 hours a day, 6 days a week, and at closing time we would either head home or to the local clubs to have "intelligent conversation" with the women. I was learning about life, and learning how to surf (but not well), however I gradually succumbed to "island fever"—and felt the itch to move on.

After about nine months or so, I thought, what was I going to do when I "grow up?" I certainly didn't want to sell jewelry for the rest of my life. I checked out the med school in Hawaii, a two-year program at the time, which required you to transfer afterwards to the mainland. I was told I had no chance of getting in because I was not yet a resident of the state. They suggested that after a year I might have a small chance.

"Just submit your MCAT scores with your transcripts next year," said the counselor at the University.

I thought to myself: "Take a standardized test again—and wait still another year? No way." As much as I wanted to go to med school, I was repeatedly told I had no chance, given that I hadn't even taken the MCAT and I was shy on one pre-med course. The old tapes were still playing—I didn't think I had the brains for med school, nor a PhD. Getting into med school or grad school required admissions tests like the MCAT or GRE. There was no way I was taking another standardized test, because I still viewed myself as the "dumb kid" and was afraid "they might find me out."

If You're Going to San Francisco

I still had an interest in psychology and had heard about a program at San Francisco State University that offered a master of science degree. They sometimes didn't require the GRE admission test if your grades were good enough from undergrad. I applied, and to my delight, eventually was accepted. It wasn't my dream of going to med school, but I thought this was a good compromise, since I always had an interest in psychology. When I told the Zales manager that I would be leaving in a month, he offered me the opportunity of being "Assistant Manager" and a huge salary increase—to $12,000 dollars a year (not bad at the time). I thanked him, turned it down, and headed to San Francisco to become a graduate student.

Every morning I'd make the drive across the Bay Bridge to attend classes in San Francisco, then drive back to my small apartment in Alameda, where I would do my reading and catch the latest episode of *Star Trek*. I was a big fan of the show. I recall one episode in which Spock said to Captain Kirk, "The only thing that is permanent in the universe is change." That line resonated for me. I had already been through so many changes— yet my life had just begun.

At SF State, I was studying how groups work together, as well as the cultural values and norms that affect decision-making. There was a general unrest in the country at the time, with the Vietnam War raging and civil rights issues at the forefront. Reading the paper one morning, it seemed to me that everything was becoming "sanitized." Political correctness was becoming en vogue. Words like "destroy the enemy" were being replaced with terms like "neutralize the enemy." This became the subject of a term paper in which I quoted Captain Kirk, who told his crew that they would take care of the Klingons, or "neutralize" them. Fortunately for me, the professor turned out to be a fan of the series.

Indiana Loans

While I was completing my master's degree, I wound up working as an intern at Kaiser Aluminum in Oakland, California. My boss, Mike Mitchell, a PhD in organizational development from Purdue University, located in West Lafayette, Indiana, encouraged me to apply to their PhD program. Armed with a letter of recommendation from him, I applied—although I had no idea how I was going to pay the tuition. The fact that all of the graduate schools required a GRE admission exam still loomed in my mind as an inevitable roadblock.

On May 22nd, 1972, I received a "provisional" letter of

acceptance from Purdue, based on my grades from UCLA and my Masters from San Francisco State University. Unbelievable as it seemed, I'd gotten into the PhD program. Not only that—they were offering me a teaching and research fellowship that would cover the $7000 tuition—about $45,000 in today's money—as well as a $400 a month stipend. There was just one catch: it was a "provisional" letter—they could not formally accept me until they received my GRE test scores. I panicked—the old tapes started playing in my head. "I can't take the test," I thought. "I'll fail. I'm not smart enough. If I take it, they'll find out who I really am."

Purdue asked me to take the next scheduled test, in June—or they wouldn't be able to admit me. I told them I couldn't take it in June, because I would be in the Army Reserves during the summer. "OK," the Purdue folks said, "we'll continue with the provisional admission, but before you get here, there's another test coming up in September. You'll need to take it." I agreed, but never registered for it. My fear was that great.

I took a huge chance and headed for Purdue University, hoping they wouldn't realize I hadn't taken the exam, and when I finally met with the advisors, nothing was mentioned.

Just before leaving San Francisco, I sold my cool '69 Datsun convertible for a more practical '69 blue Chevy Nova, which I drove cross-country to Purdue. For some reason I thought the school was closer to the East Coast than it actually was. Ok, so I wasn't great at geography. I had no idea where Lafayette, Indiana was, and didn't realize it was surrounded in large part—by cornfields.

Arriving in Indiana, I saw a little house for rent for about

$100 a month on 1713 Purdue Street (now renamed 'Perdue Street' so students would stop stealing street signs). Since my birthday was 7/13, and the street was named like the school, I thought it must be a good sign, and I quickly signed a year lease. Not having any furniture, I found some foam rubber at an old factory dumpsite and used it to make a bed. I would sleep on that foam rubber makeshift bed for the next year or so. A few bricks and boards were put together to form a bookcase, and my "office" consisted of a card table and one folding chair.

Having little money, it was frequently a choice between how much gas I could put in my Nova versus what would I have for dinner. Crackers and tomato ketchup became a favorite, and at one point I qualified for food stamps, but couldn't bring myself to accept them. I supplemented my income with other part-time jobs.

At one point, my mentor from Kaiser Aluminum showed up at Purdue for a reunion event and was shocked to see how I was living. I was fine, I assured him, and the two of us spent the evening watching the 1972 Olympics on the old black and white TV a friend had given me. There in the middle of the cornfields we watched the horrors of the Munich Olympics unfold—the kidnapping of the Israeli team. "They're all gone," sportscaster Jim McKay finally announced, and Mike and I fought back tears.

From Dunce to Doc

In many ways, Purdue was an exciting place for me. I got to do research, with access to the most advanced computer of the day—an IBM 370 which filled an entire room.

In addition to a full course load, which included classes in statistics (Purdue had an incredibly strong statistics department), I taught classes in *Group Human Relations* and *Behavioral Sciences*. I became fascinated in the psychology of group thinking and how groups work together and make decisions—this became the subject of my PhD dissertation.

I even developed a game on the subject, which was inspired by the following harrowing experience. I'd won the "Outstanding Teacher of the Year" award at Purdue in 1973, which included a $250 bonus check—paid in 10 monthly installments. One hot summer day, I brought one of my $25 dollar monthly installments to the Army Navy store and purchased a Navy life raft, which I took to a nearby lake for an afternoon of fun.

Relaxing on the raft, I was replaying in my mind how some groups seem to make "better" decisions than other groups, even though there didn't appear to be substantial differences among their members. At that moment (for reasons I'm not entirely sure of), I decided to see how long I could stay afloat if I let just a little bit of air out of each of the raft's compartments. Before I realized it, I was sinking. Paddling as fast as I could, I barely made it back to shore.

That night I lay awake thinking about my near mishap. What if I really were on a life raft in the middle of the ocean? What would I have taken with me from the sinking ship? That thought was the inception of a decision-making game that I developed, along with another grad student Bill Pasmore, called *Lost At Sea*. This game has since been used in thousands of settings around the world to teach groups of people how to make better decisions.

Lost At Sea was developed around "consensus" decision-making techniques and involves using all the available resources and opinions in the group. This was not common or accepted at the time. Standard decision-making styles of the day were usually "majority vote" or "authorization."

The game begins on a yacht in the South Pacific with somebody suddenly screaming "Fire!" As you head to the life raft, there are 15 items you can take with you and your group. You task is to rank them in order of their importance. You do this individually, then as a group.

The items included: a sextant, a shaving mirror, mosquito netting, a quart of 160 proof Puerto Rican rum, a five-gallon can of water, a case of US Army C-rations, maps of the Pacific Ocean, a floating seat cushion, a two-gallon can of gasoline, a small transistor radio, 20 square feet of opaque plastic sheeting, shark repellent, a 15-foot nylon rope, two boxes of chocolate bars, and a fishing kit.

The results of the exercise revealed that consensual decision-making techniques often improve group performance. This became one of my areas of expertise, and I wound up lecturing and publishing widely on the topic. Today, it is considered by many to be the prototype for decision-making games used by major companies to help teach their executives and employees how to make better decisions.

At the time I developed the concept I was a poor graduate student, barely making ends meet. Thus, when a book publishing company approached me to sell the story and all the rights to them for $75, I didn't hesitate. Years later, when *Lost at Sea* went on to become a bestseller, the publishing company sent me a reminder that they'd paid the $75 in full, and provided me with one copy, free of charge.

"It's OK"

I've been very fortunate to win many awards and scholarships in my life. One that I received at Purdue was from an organization called "NTL"—National Training Laboratories. It was a program that took place in Bethel, Maine during the summer of 1973. It was designed for PhD psychology students from around the country to learn new techniques in organizational development, and to participate in some "head shrinking" and group "sensitivity sessions." At the time, the biggest rage were these sessions where groups of people would sit around, led by a "facilitator," and then give feedback, often a form of "constructive" criticism, to someone else in the group.

During these sessions a pop psychology book of the day called *I'm OK, You're OK* was frequently mentioned. One guy there, a PhD in Psychology named Tom Ollerman, has remained a life-long friend. During these sessions Tom and I would often hear various "issues" from people about tragedies in their lives.

After one exhausting 8-hour marathon session, Tom blurted out "OK, enough lady. I guess I'm OK—and you're obviously not OK—but that's OK," to which we all inappropriately chuckled. And for better or worse, over the years, when one of us is telling the other about an "issue," sometimes we'll recall that line. But that's OK.

Dodging Bullets

While pursuing my PhD, I felt like something was missing. I still dreamt of becoming a physician and surgeon, and wondered if I could someday get into medical school. At Purdue, I did well, receiving all As and just one B, earning recognition by national honor societies, and other awards. I enjoyed research and teaching, and my dissertation wound up being published in a prestigious journal. I already had a number of job offers lined up when my advisor, Dr. Donald King, called me into his office. The final shoe was about to drop.

"You've completed all the requirements for the program, and excelled," he began, adding that I had passed all my written and oral exams, as well as being selected Outstanding Teacher of the Year. "However," Dr. King said, "there's one more thing that's been pointed out to me by the Dean's Office. I'm sure it's a mistake, but we can't seem to find your scores from the GRE exam—you know, the one that you took to apply for Purdue."

My heart sank. Had they finally "found me out?" He asked me if I could "re-take" the test the next month, just for good measure. As he saw the horrified expression on my face, we both realized the absurdity of it. However, the Dean was strongly encouraging me to take it.

I explained that I had completed everything, and that this was an admissions test, not a graduate requirement. Also, I pleaded, I simply didn't have the extra $25 for the test fee. After listening to my argument, all parties realized how ridiculous it was for me to take the admissions exam at this point. Once again, the "dunce" had slipped under the radar.

Moving On

Several months later, I began my first job as a PhD, as an organizational development psychologist at Kaiser Hospitals in Oakland, California. I remember leaving Indiana, driving back through the cornfields in my blue Chevy Nova, returning to Northern California to start my new position.

Eventually, I would become Director of Staff Development for a number of Kaiser Permanente hospitals in the Bay Area, but my dream of becoming a medical doctor would continue to resonate in my mind. I would soon find myself slipping under the radar again to achieve this elusive goal.

4

THE OVAL OFFICE

I was disappointed when I arrived in Oakland and learned that I would be working in Kaiser's Alameda building, with the rest of the psychologists and consultants—not in the "big building" in Oakland with the company executives. That feeling of disappointment soon faded, however, when I discovered that the building overlooked both the Alameda Bay and San Francisco Bay, with a number of great restaurants within walking distance. I wasn't in the cornfields anymore.

Soon after I started, I was called to lead a big meeting at the Oakland building. Seated around the massive conference table that day were all the company's VPs, with the president, known to all as "KTS," seated at the head of the table. Karl T. Stiles was a huge man. At six foot four, he was an imposing figure, with a big booming voice that resonated in the minds of all as he spoke. He was dressed in a suit, as always, and every time he opened his mouth, the response from around the table was "Yes, KTS."

I was in the middle of my presentation on team building and decision-making strategies, flip cards in hand, when KTS broke in and started talking about his new strategies on the subject. I had been talking about the "organic team approach," using the *Lost at Sea* exercise I had developed at Purdue to show how all resources could be used to get the different perspectives.

KTS would have none of that. He was a "chain of command" guy. He rarely got any feedback about what was going on, but that was the price he paid. Folks were just too nervous to disagree with him. When he was finished, he asked everyone what they thought. One by one, they chimed in with the usual, "Yes, KTS—great thinking, KTS," and so on.

When it got back to me, I disagreed. Suddenly you could hear a pin drop. Across the room, one of the VPs was making hand signals for me to cut it out. After the meeting, KTS called me into his office.

"Nemiroff," he said, addressing me in his big booming voice, "don't ever correct me in front of my VPs. Now sit down."

I took a seat in front of his desk.

"You don't have a mortgage, do you?"

"No," I answered."

"And you don't have kids."

"No I don't."

"Good. So I can use you as a resource that will give me some good, honest feedback."

KTS wasn't asking me, he was telling me. He said he was going to be moving me to the main building in Oakland, to the office right next to his. Initially, I wasn't crazy about the idea because everyone there would see me as a possible "conduit" to the boss and somebody not to be trusted. But KTS insisted. He handed me a catalogue and told me to pick out whatever furniture I wanted for my new office.

Dr. Nemiroff named to P.S.I. post as D.S.D.

Paul Nemiroff, Ph.D., has been appointed Director of Staff Development for Permanente Services, Inc. In this new position he will serve as consultant to PSI departments, assisting them in improving organizational effectiveness, and will be coordinator of PSI management development activities.

Dr. Nemiroff, formerly an Organization Development consultant for General Foods, earned his Ph.D. in Administrative Sciences from Purdue University and his Master's degree in Industrial/Organizational Psychology from San Francisco University. He also has taught courses in Behavioral and Administrative Sciences at Purdue.

July 25, 1975

Kaiser Permanente newsletter

As Director of Staff Development, I had what they called "The Oval Office," with a spectacular view of the city of Oakland. It was just me, KTS, and the chief medical officer on that floor. I went from drinking coffee out of Styrofoam™ cups to having my own secretary bringing me fancy teas, coffee and cookies on fine China, and a huge salary increase. Suddenly it was, "Yes, Dr. Nemiroff."

My job was to conduct training sessions for everyone from vice presidents on down, to help them communicate with their employees and make them better decision makers and problem solvers.

Frankly, I felt like I was way over my head. I'd never been in the business world before. All I knew was the theory I'd picked up during my PhD work, and what I had gleaned from the studies I'd done for various organizations. I was only 25, and I didn't have the in-the-trenches experience.

The same guys who wouldn't even talk to me before I got promoted suddenly wanted to be my best friend. I was viewed as a conduit of information to KTS. People would feed me things hoping it would get back to him.

The real problem was that within six months of starting the job, I was bored to death. I asked myself: "What have I done? Is this it?" Again, something was missing.

I didn't have to get in until 9:30 a.m. in the morning—at 4:30 p.m. I'd go play handball. Then there were the two-hour lunches these guys took. And they drank a ton back then. These were two and three martini lunches. I mean, the work ethic wasn't exactly stellar at the time. It was before computers and cell phones and people just disappeared for half the day.

I was bored out of my mind, and I started thinking maybe now was the time that I try to get into medical school. The dream of becoming a doctor had never left me, not from childhood. I still wanted to be one of those men in the white coats, helping people. The only thing standing in my way was my lack of confidence. I just didn't think I was smart enough. That—and the MCATs. Every medical school required MCAT scores for admission. If I took them, I'd be found out for the "dunce" I was. But now I had my BA, MS, and PhD with pretty much straight As all the way through graduate school, and all these accolades. Maybe I had a shot after all—if I could just find a school that didn't require the MCATs.

I had to try. I had had all kinds of job offers after Purdue—Union Carbide, Texas Instruments. Why had I chosen Kaiser Permanente? Because it was a medical institution and I got to be around doctors and work with them, which made me want to be one even more. If I could just slip through the cracks one more time…

I was short a biochemistry course, so I quietly enrolled in a night class at a local state college while I started looking into schools. The University of Miami looked like a possibility. They had a new program to get people with PhDs through four years of medical school in just two years. That sounded great. I applied and they flew me across the country for an interview.

After flying back and forth twice on their nickel and staying at the Chairman's house, I thought I had it in the bag. Not so. It turned out they had never admitted a PhD with a psychology background before—they had always gone for engineers. I became an alternate, in case someone dropped out, and they encouraged me to apply again the next year. But that was enough. I figured I probably wasn't smart enough anyway to do it in two years. So I started applying to a bunch of medical schools, hoping they would overlook the missing MCATs.

I had to tell KTS, who was actually very supportive, of my

becoming a medical doctor. I sent out many, many applications.

Eventually, I managed to get an interview at UCLA, partly because I had received my BA with honors from there, and I already had a Masters degree, and a PhD and was working in the medical system at Kaiser Permanente. On the flight down from San Francisco, I picked up a business magazine and began reading an article about the state of healthcare at the time. It had a lot of statistics about various funding issues, particularly Medicare. I read the entire article and was amazed the next day when the first person to interview me at UCLA pulled the same magazine out of his desk and asked if I paid any attention to current events in medicine.

"I try to keep up," I said.

He then turned to the very article I had read on the plane and started to ask me questions. He didn't like that I worked at Kaiser Permanente—HMOs were viewed as socialized medicine at the time, by some. But his entire demeanor changed when I started citing chapter, verse, and statistics from the very article he was questioning me on.

"You are obviously a very well-rounded young man," he said. "You seem knowledgeable about current affairs. We may call you for another interview, but first you need to take the MCATs and a biochemistry course.

I informed him that I had already taken the biochemistry course, and that I intended to take the MCATs, though I had no intention of doing so.

After additional interviews, months passed. Then came the letter that would forever change my life.

"Congratulations," it read, "you've been accepted into medical school at UCLA. In order to secure your position, you need to remit $50 immediately." After rechecking the envelope to make sure it had been delivered to the right person, I quickly sent them a check. The MCATs were never mentioned again. I later learned that at the discretion of the Dean very rare exceptions could be made.

When I told KTS about my good fortune, he was very supportive. He offered me a $10,000 no-obligation scholarship, asking only that I would consider coming back and working for him after I became a physician. "There are no strings attached to this," he insisted, "only my hope that I can have another doctor in my pocket." (smile)

Initially I refused the money, but KTS insisted and had the accountant set it up legitimately as a scholarship fund. Without that ten grand, I probably couldn't have gone to UCLA. There was no way. I was tapped out on all my student loans. His act of generosity changed my life.

5

FIRST DO NO HARM

My arrival at UCLA was the fulfillment of a lifelong dream—I couldn't believe I was there. Forget the bellbottom jeans and the striped t-shirt I wore to orientation. It was the 1970s and we all looked a little goofy in the casual wear of the day. The truth is, I was in awe of the place.

I was going to be studying human anatomy with some of the most renowned anatomy professors in the world—men like Dr. Carmine Clemente who literally wrote the book on modern human anatomy, and others who contributed to *Grant's Atlas of Anatomy.*

Here I was sitting among the best of the best. Thousands and thousands had applied, and only about a hundred-forty of us had gotten in. Everybody around me was in the top one percentile. I was pinching myself, saying, "How the heck did I ever get in here?" Somebody must have been watching over me.

The work hit me like a wave—hours and hours of reading and memorizing, from biochemistry to physiology to anatomy. Book after book, day after day, voluminous amounts of material were presented to us. It seemed impossible to learn all of it.

The first two years were crazy. In addition to attending classes, I was working as a part-time consultant psychologist to Kaiser Permanente in the area, just to make ends meet. In order to cope with all the reading, I started using various mnemonics to try to memorize things. One of the devices I developed for rounds I called "C-MINT," or "Candy-MINT," which covered every possible cause of any disease or situation. It went like this:

C=Congenital or hereditary causes.

M=Metabolic causes, e.g. diabetes.

I=anything due to Infections or viruses.

N=Neoplastic, or anything having to do with cancer or a tumor.

T=Trauma, or accident-related conditions.

Whenever the attending physician asked what might be the cause of Mrs. Jones' kidney failure, I could quickly spout off the possible causes of her malady, even if I didn't know for certain. This type of word association, as well as visual imagery, served me well on rounds.

Another mnemonic device I developed was called "IHOP." I used this acronym to remember the four basic indications for surgery, as opposed to the "watch-and-wait." If any of these situations were present, it was time to operate:

I=Intractable (unbearable) pain, not responding to medications

H=Hemorrhage (severe bleeding)

O=Obstruction (of the intestine, or twisting of the bowel)

P=Perforation (a hole in the stomach or intestine)

That and about 10,000 flash cards I developed for every subject helped me through the bulk of my studies.

Color Blindness—Revisited

However, I had no such mnemonic devices to assist me when my colorblindness came back to haunt me in the parasitology lab. For this class, we had to scrape feces onto slides and then look at the slides under the microscope to try to identify the parasites. I'd had some earlier difficulties in cadaver studies, because cadavers weren't like live flesh with all the blood pulsing through it. And cadaver nerves don't "light up" like the white, glistening nerves in a live body.

One of the professors had commented then that I was going to have a real problem becoming a surgeon because of my colorblindness—that I wasn't going to be able to distinguish between the various tissue colors. That was a real hit in the head. I figured I'd do my best. At the very least, I was going to be a doctor.

I managed to make it through the cadaver labs studying structures. The parasitology lab in my second year, however, turned out to be a greater challenge. I was having a real problem distinguishing between the various stains used to distinguish different parasites, like aniline blue and Congo red. The staining was a very time-consuming, arduous process, with all the different stains and colors. I was having a tough time—the blues, greens and Congo reds all seemed to blend together. The fact that I was missing a lot of labs, because I was working my part-time consulting job at Kaiser to make ends meet, didn't help any.

Just before the final exam, the teaching assistant came up to me and said, "Nemiroff, there's no way you're going to pass the test. You've missed too much lab time."

Undaunted, I headed for the UCLA bookstore where I found a very expensive parasitology book with colored plates and descriptions below, and, more importantly, the various shapes of the parasites. I figured if I could just remember the shapes I wouldn't get lost in the merging colors.

I studied that book day and night, memorizing every shape of every parasite. I wound up getting one of the highest grades in the class, much to the consternation of the teaching assistant. Once again, I had slipped through the cracks; now I look at it another way: Overcoming obstacles in life. The book even had a two-week return policy on it, so I was able to get my $100 bucks back. The dean, hearing that I had missed so many classes, set me up with a $10,000 loan so I wouldn't miss any more instruction, though I would be paying back that 12 percent loan for many years. It was either that or quit medical school.

Making Rounds

During my third and fourth years at UCLA, I began meeting with patients on the wards. My first "work-up" was a middle-aged woman who had undergone chemotherapy for her metastatic breast cancer at a local hospital that was affiliated with UCLA. By the time I was assigned to do a history and a physical on her, she was bald from the chemotherapy and very weak. But the first day I appeared at the doorway to her room, she welcomed me in with a smile and warmth. She must have sensed my nervousness and was doing her best to make me feel at ease. I remember asking her, as I was instructed to, what it was like to have cancer.

"It just changes everything," she told me. "It changes all your priorities. It changes the way you view the world." While I didn't know it at the time, one day I would learn this perspective firsthand.

She wanted to fight. She was afraid of leaving her family. But the thing that struck me most was her kindness and compassion for me, as a new doctor in training. Even with my countless questions, she was kind and patient with me every time I came to see her.

Every week I looked forward to visiting and talking with her about her treatments, and whatever else she wanted to discuss. She was befriending me, teaching me the questions to ask a person who has cancer—like "How are you feeling today—on a scale of one to ten?" I got that from her. She said there were days that were a negative ten, and then there were days when she might feel as good as a five.

She was just very kind.

And then I remember the day I walked in and the sheets were changed and she wasn't there. It was a clean, freshly made bed. I asked the nurse where she'd been transferred.

"Oh, no," she replied. "She passed away last night."

I was confused. I thought she'd been doing better.

"These things just happen," the nurse said.

She saw I was visibly grieving because someone I had made a connection with was gone.

"It was just her time," the nurse said to me, reassuringly.

I knew then why I was training to be a doctor, and I began to understand what it meant to be a doctor. It wasn't all about tests, or questions, or probing. It was truly about the human spirit and the kind of doctor-patient relationship that we all hope for. We all want a physician who is caring and compassionate, technically competent, yes—but also a doctor who truly gives something back to their patients.

At this moment in my training, I wanted to be all of these things, because I didn't want to see other people going through the misery this poor woman had gone through.

Training to be a good surgeon is a real balancing act, because this is where technical expertise and the ability to hold onto one's wits in times of crisis are tested to the limits.

My own baptism by fire occurred during my OB/GYN rotation at Torrance-UCLA hospital. I chose Torrance because there was a need for Spanish-speaking doctors, and also because I was going to have the opportunity to do more there than I would have at hospitals where the medical students didn't interact as much with patients. At Torrance, I got to start IVs, do things like "spinal taps," and assist in deliveries from the beginning.

One night I was doing whatever they needed me to do, starting IVs, monitoring women in labor and so on, when they rolled in this lady. She was fully dilated. It wasn't her first baby, so she was going to deliver fast. I was told to prepare her for a pudendal bloc—an injection of a local anesthetic to relieve the pain the woman was going to experience during delivery.

I was speaking Spanish to her just outside of the delivery room, telling her to just breathe and don't push yet. There were a bunch of women lined up about to have babies and the residents were all busy. All of a sudden, as I was speaking with this woman, a little foot "popped out," and the monitor on the woman's belly showed that the baby was in fetal distress. I started paging the chief resident. Then the nurse came running in.

"It's a breach," she said, meaning the baby was coming out feet-first instead of headfirst. She STAT paged the chief resident while we rolled the woman into the OR.

A moment later the chief resident came in, looked directly at me, and said, "Do exactly what I tell you to do."

I nodded.

"We've got to do a crash C-section," she told me. "I want you to hold the "idiot sticks" (the retractors that hold the belly open during the C-section) and don't say or do anything except what I tell you to do. You got that Nemiroff?"

I nodded again.

The doctor didn't inject any local anesthesia or anything—she whiffed the patient down with some nitrous oxide via a mask, then she slit the pregnant woman's belly open. There was bleeding all around, on everything.

"Here," she said, handing me the retractors and repositioning them to keep the woman's belly open, "hold these and don't move."

Then she started clamping off bleeding vessels left and right, not bothering tying knots on anything, because we were trying to get the kid out, who was dying, and the lady was bleeding out. She was clamping only the big vessels, letting the little ones go. There was no time. We had only minutes before this kid started to go brain dead.

Then the chief resident reached into the uterus, and in one motion pulled the kid out and handed it to a nurse.

Then she took hold of the retractors and said to me, "I'll hold the retractors, clamp the cord and double clamp it. Then cut it.

She actually took the retractors away from me for a second to give me the opportunity to clamp and cut the cord.

Then she handed me back one retractor, while she held the other, and we started cleaning up the bleeding. A nurse came in to help. The woman and the baby both did fine. I was just in awe of this chief resident's skill. She was amazing during this big crash C-section.

The hours were long, though. At times, I was there 24 hours straight, then 12 hours off. The workload was insane. I slept at the hospital. They put us in trailers out back with bunk beds—there was no air conditioning and it often reached over a hundred degrees during the summer. It was hard work, but I wouldn't have wanted to be anywhere else.

The Making of a Surgeon

It was during my rotations through the various surgical specialties that one of my professors told me I had "the hands of a surgeon." I found myself excelling in surgical specialties, learning how to operate and sew, how to tie a knot or "throw a suture," mostly in the dog labs (which were part of a surgeon's training—on dogs from the pound that were going to be euthanized). As my skills grew, for the first time I started thinking, maybe, just maybe I can do this.

In many instances, surgeons are not typically known for their great bedside manner. The good ones are known for their decisiveness and their skill. In William Nolan's classic book *The Making of a Surgeon* he wrote that surgeons are "complete doctors" because they not only can prescribe pills, they can also "cut" when required. The old saying, "A chance to cut is a chance to cure" is something I first heard at UCLA.

An old joke comes to mind. It has to do with the differences in personalities among surgeons, family doctors, and internists. It begins with three doctors going hunting.

The first doctor, a very practical family physician, hears what he thinks is a duck and says to himself, "It looks like a duck, sounds like a duck, must be a duck." Bang! He takes a shot.

The second doctor, a more probing internist, says, "Looks like a duck, sounds like a duck, but let's order some tests and rule out turkey, pigeon, swallow, and swan." Finally, he surmises it's a duck, and Bang! He takes his shot.

The third doctor, a surgeon, hears a quack and immediately lets loose with his machine gun—Bang-Bang-Bang! Then he says to the other two, "What the hell was that?"

In a crude way, this joke sums up some of the differences in the personalities of various specialists. As I later came to learn, there was some truth to the surgeon's reputation for arrogance, brashness, and thriving on immediate feedback when it comes to decision-making. As with fighter pilots, there is a certain type of personality that is required to be a surgeon—to act decisively and keep your composure under extreme pressure. It's not easy when a child's mangled body is brought into the ER, and it's YOU that has to put the pieces back together again.

PhDs and MDs (especially surgeons) have quite divergent thinking processes. Therefore, someone who has both a PhD and an MD, like myself, may have some psychic conflict when it comes to decision-making. I found I was able to compartmentalize those processes and be decisive when I needed to be. In the OR, you don't have the luxury of building consensus or conducting a majority vote—e.g. the *Lost At Sea* game that I developed at Purdue—the surgeon is the one who has to make the sometime life-and-death decisions—right now.

Listen—Don't Assume

During my dermatology rotation, I noticed a man sitting in the waiting room wearing an ascot around his neck. A strange hose-like tube, which appeared to be made of skin, protruded from his chest and was sutured into his eye. Not surprisingly, the other patients in the waiting room were taking care to avoid him. Later I came to understand that this was something called a "pedicle flap" used in reconstructive procedures. But at the time it just looked very peculiar to me.

One of the residents told me to do a "work-up," a history and a physical on this man. I greeted the man when he came into the examining room and introduced myself as a physician in training.

"What exactly happened?" I asked, pointing to the flap of tissue coming out of his chest. "I'm sure it must be very uncomfortable for you."

"Are you crazy?" the man responded. "Don't you know why I'm here? I have this giant pimple on my forehead that won't go away. I'm not here about this other stuff."

Then I looked at the man's forehead and saw this 1/4-inch lesion that appeared to be the least of his problems. But that's what he was concerned about. That's when I came to understand an old axiom in medicine—"Listen to the patient" (and for newer docs in training…stop looking at your cell phone and computer) and they'll tell you what's wrong with them, and many times they'll give you the diagnosis. Listen—don't assume.

The Royal Free

During my fourth year at UCLA, I was offered the opportunity to do a month-long rotation in England at the Royal Free Hospital. There I would work with two of the most prestigious ENT surgeons in the United Kingdom—Mr. Ballantine and Mr. Groves. They had written a classic textbook about ear, nose and throat disorders, and surgery. In England at the time, you didn't refer to a Surgeon as "Doctor"—that was considered an insult.

They were "Misters" in the hospitals, to distinguish themselves from non-surgical physicians. This was the expectation of how they were addressed.

On my first day in London, I took a taxi which appeared to be an ancient Rolls Royce. I asked the taxi driver to take me to the Royal Free Hospital, and he laughed and said, "Royal Free? It's anything but free, mate." The Royal Free Hospital was like the Cedars-Sinai of London. This was an unparalleled opportunity for me to see another country, learn something about their culture, and realize there were limitations to socialized medicine.

One day while in the "Operating Theater" (as they called the Operating Room), the surgeon, who had just filleted open a man's head, casually said, "It's 4 p.m.—tea time, let's take a break." He placed a wet "lap sponge" over the wound and left the patient under the care of the anesthesiologist. Off we went, clicking down the hallway wearing our wooden Dutch-boy-like surgical shoes, to have tea. These wooden surgical shoes were one of the other oddities of the Operating Theater. A cart provided all sorts of tea and crumpets, and the docs sat around in the lounge enjoying their 20-minute break. Seeing the astonished look on my face, the surgeon said to me, "We don't operate here like you do in the States—we're civilized."

The surgeon's lounge was quite unique. It featured a bar and smoking area, and seemed more like a hotel than a hospital. Reportedly, no one ever drank while on duty, but it was certainly a different culture.

One of the surgeons shared with me how little he earned in the socialized system. They were taxed 80% on the pound. Rather than strict payment, they would sometimes use a barter system. I recall one patient who traded a Persian rug for his rhinoplasty (nose job).

One aspect of socialized medicine that was disturbing to me was that Registrars, surgical residents in England, had to wait for someone to die or quit before they could get an appointment at a hospital. Some of these Registrars had been waiting for nine years for an appointment. Because of this policy, their work ethic seemed to be different than in the States, where we were on call every other night and stayed until the job was done. Some Registrars were leaving at four or five in the afternoon. One Registrar who had been there for nine years (an R9) asked me, "Why should we work so hard? The patients will all queue-up tomorrow. And if they really have a problem, they can always queue-up at the Urgency Center."

With socialized medicine, people would take a number on the National Registrar directory—and then wait. But what if little Johnny needs a tonsillectomy, right now? The doctor would say, "He'll have to queue-up on the National Registrar, and it could be 18 months." The running joke was, if a mother inquired to the doctor, "What if we go around the system, and go private?"— meaning that she would pay for it herself. The surgeon would then respond, "Has Johnny eaten breakfast today?"

Match Day

I returned to UCLA to finish up medical school, and decided on my specialty—Oto-rhino-laryngology, also known as Ear, Nose and Throat Surgery, and Head & Neck Surgery. The decision for this specialty was based in part on the influence of some of my amazing mentors, including Dr. Paul Ward and Dr. Dale Rice.

Toward the end of your final year in medical school, there is something called the infamous "Match Day." Students try to match with various programs around the country for their particular specialty. Matching with your first choice is a big deal. You find out where you're going on that specific day, when a sealed envelope is delivered to you.

Where you go for your residency—which could be nearly any hospital in the country—determines a lot about your career. I was fairly certain that I would get my first choice for general surgery, which was required to do before being able to place in Head & Neck surgery. As I carefully opened the sealed envelope, to my delight, there were no surprises. I was headed to Cedars-Sinai for general surgery, a premiere hospital in Beverly Hills known worldwide for their high quality of care, and the many celebrities who are treated there.

Besides the thousands of hours of book work and classes, the four years at UCLA as a med student included many tasks: delivering babies, starting IVs, doing spinal taps, drawing blood, doing histories and physicals on patients, taking patients to X-ray, examining their urine under a microscope, and essentially examining, at one time or another, every orifice in the human body. Equally important was learning about the morals, ethics, and philosophical aspects of being a doctor. I hope these values are still being instilled into our young doctors of today. The ultimate rule of medicine that I learned was—"First, Do No Harm."

6

GUCCI GENERAL

After four years of medical school, the day finally arrived. As one friend said, with my PhD and now MD, I was "Doctor-Doctor" or "Doctor-squared." Maybe I wasn't so dumb after all. From med student on June 30th to "Medical Doctor" on July 1st, this was where the rubber meets the road. Welcome to "The Year of the Intern."

All over the country on July 1st, brand new interns (doctors) were beginning their first day at the hospital. The running joke was: "it wasn't a good day to get sick," given the influx of all the green interns.

On June 30th, the night before my first scheduled day of work as a "real doctor," I gathered with my fellow interns at Cedars-Sinai Medical Center in Beverly Hills, California (aka "Gucci General") to meet with the director of surgical residencies. There were eight of us in the room that afternoon waiting to hear where in the hospital each of us was going to be assigned, when the director received a handwritten message informing him that one of the more senior residents had called in "sick" that night. Hence, one of us would be starting our internship—*immediately*.

The Director's eyes scoured the room, then fell on me.

"You're Nemiroff, aren't you?" he said.

"Yes, sir," I replied.

"Congratulations, you're starting right now in the SICU."

Paul Nemiroff, M.D.
U.C.L.A.
School of Medicine

Cedars-Sinai yearbook (1981)

The Surgical Intensive Care Unit was one of the most intense places to start.

"Do you have a problem with this?" the Director asked.

"No sir," I said, "but I don't have any clothes." Some of the other interns grinned, happy not to be picked and surprised at my silly answer.

"We'll provide you with scrubs and a toothbrush. Now get busy. Congratulations, you're on call as of NOW."

That was it. I threw on some scrubs, the secretary handed me a beeper and told me to start making rounds with the attending doctor. Then, shortly after the attending went home and the chief resident was tied up with something else, I got STAT paged—"Doctor Nemiroff, SICU, Code Blue." A man was dying. They had code teams, but they were also busy doing something else.

So there I was, running into the room. The dying man I remember was in bed six. He was about 70 and he was in the middle of a heart attack, and then a full arrest. His heart had stopped beating and one of the nurses was rubbing the paddles together. Then she handed them to me. Suddenly I was shocking this man with the paddles—he responded, at least for a moment. At the same time, many things can occur during a "code."

"May I suggest a back board?" the senior nurse said. You don't want to compress a patient's chest while they are on a soft bed. You need to put a hard board underneath them.

"Back board, yes," I replied.

"Chest compression, doctor??"

One of the nurses was already doing it.

"Yes," I said.

"Perhaps an AMP of epinephrine?" She was already putting it into the IV.

"Yes," I said. "One amp of epy—STAT."

He was starting to come back, but he was exhibiting all sorts of arrhythmias.

"May I recommend an amp of lidocaine?" the nurse said.

"Yes, lidocaine."

Next was an amp of calcium gluconate.

"Yes," I responded.

I was "officially" running the code for cardiac arrest, but she was running me through it.

Finally, the code team arrived and transferred the patient to the cardiac care unit, where he recovered.

"You're going to make it too," the nurse said, smiling.

"How do you know?" I asked.

"Because you listen."

This was the beginning of my respect for well-trained ICU nurses. Also, if you want any chance of getting some sleep at night, you'd better "make nice" with the nursing staff.

Five minutes later, I was STAT-paged to the ER where a man had extreme abdominal pain. I examined him and could tell his was a classic case of acute appendicitis. If his appendix ruptured, he would get peritonitis and potentially die. His white count was at 20,000—very high, and a sign of infection—and he also had a "rigid" (rock-hard) abdomen—which meant I had to get him to the OR right away.

There's a trick when you're examining someone who you suspect has appendicitis. Besides all the exams and tests—you ask them what their favorite food is, then offer to bring them some. His was ice cream. When I asked him if he wanted some, and he had said, "No, I don't want anything," there's a good chance he may have something wrong.

At this point in my training, I wasn't experienced in performing appendectomies, so I called the chief resident. He arrived and did his own exam, feeling the tenderness in lower border of the man's abdomen.

"Good call, Nemiroff," he said.

We rushed him to the OR.

I scrubbed in for the appendectomy and was assisting, mainly holding the "idiot sticks," or retractors, to allow the surgeon to see more clearly into the belly. At the end of the case, I was allowed to sew up the incision—an honor for an intern. I wrote post-operative orders, and along with the attending surgeon, spoke with the family. No sooner had I finished speaking with the family when my beeper went off again. This time it was a young child in the ER with something stuck in his throat. It was call after call after call, all night long. Sleep was out of the question.

It was 6 a.m. when I walked downstairs to make rounds with the attending surgeons and give feedback to my fellow interns as to what had happened that night. As I saw the faces of my colleagues, who had not yet been on call or had their "trial by fire," I could see some of the fear in their eyes. But my fear had dissipated, at least for the time being.

I started my briefing like a bedtime story—"Our sleepy little story begins with Patient X..." That would become a catchphrase for me on morning rounds for years to come. I was on the journey of a lifetime—the making of a surgeon.

Celebrity Central

At Cedars-Sinai, we had our share of celebrities. No matter how famous or macho they were, most celebrities in the hospital, in their gowns, stripped of everything, just wanted what everyone wants when sick and suffering—someone who shows kindness and caring.

One day I couldn't understand why a female resident was so willing to do one of my work-ups on a patient. Though exhausted, I couldn't help but be suspicious of her motives, which became quite clear to me the minute we walked through the door of the patient's room. There on the bed was legendary actor Rock Hudson. He had just had his chest prepped and shaved for a cardiac procedure. He was a handsome man with a big beautiful set of teeth as he smiled. "Hey Doc," he said, as we approached the bed, "Now I know what a plucked chicken feels like."

One of the nurses told me late one night that Johnny Carson's famous sidekick Ed McMahon, a patient at Gucci General, wanted to see me. I asked her if he needed something to help him sleep. "No," she said, he just wanted to talk to me. As it turned out, he didn't have any socks, and he said he needed socks at night to help him sleep. Well, it was 2 a.m. and there were no stores open, so I gladly offered my gym socks to him, which were in my locker and only "slightly" used. Mr. McMahon was very appreciative and later invited me to *The Tonight Show* where I sat in the famous Green Room and Control Room, and met with the guests and producers of the show.

One day Tommy Lasorda, long-time manager of the LA Dodgers, came into Cedars and shook my hand, asking, "Where's Hank?" I wondered who he was talking about, since he had just walked into my father's room—who was a patient there at the time. Apparently he'd gotten the room number wrong, and was searching for Henry Fonda.

Weeks earlier, my Dad had called me after reading an article in *Reader's Digest*. The article mentioned possible causes of blood in the stool, and my Dad asked me if I knew anything about it, as he'd had this problem. He told me he'd gone to his HMO and was told they would do more tests in the weeks and months to come and not to be worried.

I told him to get to Cedars immediately and I set him up with a top doctor for a colonoscopy. He had the procedure on a Thursday, and it turned out to be cancer. He was scheduled for surgery on Monday and told to come in Sunday night.

As fate would have it, I was the intern the night of his admission. I checked on him all that night as he took the necessary beverages to help clear his intestines. (One was called "Go LYTELY™"—however its name was quite an understatement.)

Surgery the next day went well. I had asked not to be present during my Father's surgery—and the attending surgeons agreed. It's almost never a good idea to be involved in surgery with a family member since it can cloud your judgment. A day or so later, his lab report came back as "Duke's B," which was good news—it hadn't spread to the lymph nodes. It was strange but comforting, making rounds each day and visiting him with the other doctors. Changing the abdominal dressings made me feel closer to him than I ever had before.

My brother Art and sister-in-law Ute came to visit my Dad each day. Art said to me, "You were working here late last night. What time did you get home?" I replied, "I didn't. I've been here 24 hours straight." Art now understood how hard I was working. Most people have no idea of the intensity of a surgical resident's schedule, with frequent 100-plus hour workweeks.

Drug Deal Gone Wrong

After having been up nearly 24 hours, I was heading home when suddenly my beeper went off. I wasn't on call, but all the other interns were tied up, and I was expected to respond. The adrenaline rush kicked in, and after a few expletives were uttered,

I rushed back to the ER. I was told there was a woman with a gunshot wound to her head. Pieces of her skull were fractured like a broken plate. They had already put a tube in her to help her breathe, and a neurosurgeon was assessing the situation, saying "Dr. Nemiroff, you are assisting me in this surgery—call the OR and let's go."

Once prepped in the OR, the neurosurgeon began pulling bits of her skull out from her brain. In assessing the situation, it turns out it wasn't a gunshot wound at all, but rather, it appeared she had been bludgeoned with an axe. At the time, my job was primarily to hold the infamous idiot sticks, or retractors, so the surgeon could see what he was doing.

The woman survived the surgery and was taken to the ICU. After 24 hours of non-stop stress, I was about to collapse from fatigue. Hours later I discovered that this woman was at the center of a horrific murder scandal. The "stinking media" (as those of us in the media sometimes call it) announced that there was one sole survivor from a number of killings in Laurel Canyon over a drug deal gone bad. Moments after this announcement, there was a bomb threat at Cedars, probably because she was the one person who could potentially identify the murderer, if she woke up.

SWAT teams initially appeared, then for weeks plain-clothes policemen guarded the hospital corridors. The only comical part occurred one day when one of the doctors came up to check on the lady. He was wearing tennis clothes and had a tennis racquet wrapped in a case. The policeman asked him who he was, and he replied that he didn't have his ID with him. So the policeman asked me if I knew who he was.

The guy was one of our attending doctors, and I was exhausted from a long night, so I jokingly said, "I don't know who this guy is." The police immediately threw him up against the wall. It was only when I told them, "Just kidding, guys—he's a doctor," that they let him go. The attending doctor was not amused, and later said to me, "Nemiroff, don't mess with the 'boys in blue'— and I'll see you in my office in five."

Pick of the Litter

One of the most colorful patients to come my way at Cedars-Sinai was a fellow we'll call "Rodney," who was rushed into the ER one night with a gunshot wound to his arm. He was dressed flamboyantly, with multiple gold chains, high boots, and a big purple hat with a feather. Accompanying him was an entourage of "professional" women who seemed genuinely concerned for his well-being.

When asked, Rodney explained that he didn't have health insurance and he wanted to pay cash. With a snap of his fingers, the ladies produced rolls of hundred dollar bills from various areas of their skimpy outfits. After his surgery, Rodney was very appreciative. "Doc," he said, "you've been real good to me. To show my appreciation—you get the pick of the litter. It's on the house." I thanked Rodney, but politely declined. "Just another day of saving lives."

You've Got Some Nerve

During my rotations at Cedars-Sinai, I was fortunate to have some of the best surgeons as mentors, as well as be exposed to the whole gamut of medical emergencies—including 12-hour cancer surgeries. One of my great mentors was Dr. Al Katz, an outstanding thyroid surgeon. Al Katz was the "Thyroid King." One day we were doing a surgery and he said to me that you have to be careful because sometimes the nerve serving the larynx bifurcates (splits) into two branches.

"It's a rare occurrence," he said, but the bifurcation is not protected by cartilage, so you have to be careful not to cut one of the branches. Cutting the nerves—and it did happen—resulted in the patient losing speech, or having a terrible voice, at a minimum.

Suddenly, I started seeing the nerve 'split' on nearly every other case we did. Every time I saw it, I would point it out to him and say, "Look, there's another bifurcation." I'd been there for five days and I was seeing all these bifurcations that no one ever talked about. And each time I pointed it out, Al would say, "You're right. I didn't see that. How did you see it?"

"I don't know," I'd say. "It just jumps out at me."

"Well, we should do a study on it," he said.

How was I able to see these bifurcations in so many patients when nobody else could? During World War II, the US Army found that colorblind persons could "see" camouflage colors, where those with normal color vision couldn't. They used the colorblind troops in planes, as they did with helicopters in Vietnam, to spot camouflaged tanks and artillery. So here I was spotting nerve bifurcations nobody else was seeing.

Dr. Katz and I started looking at this RLN (recurrent laryngeal nerve), measuring how far the split was occurring from the larynx and how often we were seeing it on the right or left side. Over the next couple months, we conducted and published a study, reporting on scores of patients, and 153 nerves. [American Journal of Surgery—October 1982—144 (4): 466-9 *Extra-laryngeal divisions of the recurrent laryngeal nerve—Surgical and clinical significance.* Nemiroff PM, Katz AD]

Years later, we co-authored another study on nearly 1200 nerves examined. [American Journal of Surgery, March 1993—59 (3): 188-91. *Anastomoses and bifurcations of the recurrent laryngeal nerve—report of 1177 nerves visualized.* Katz AD, Nemiroff PM].

We were amazed at how often it was occurring—over half the time—yet the classical textbooks of the day discussed this more as an anatomical rarity. That changed after our publications.

"This is amazing," Dr. Katz said. He added a few touches to my write-up then we submitted it to the American College of Surgeons and to the Society of Head & Neck Surgeons. I won first place in the nationwide competition of the Society of Head and Neck Surgeons annual awards for the paper—*"Extra-laryngeal Divisions of the Recurrent Laryngeal Nerve: Surgical and Clinical Significance."*

The prize included a $500 check. When you're making $12,500 a year as a surgical intern, and working 120 hours a week, that's a big deal. They flew me to Marco Island, Florida to present it at the annual meeting. Suddenly Cedars-Sinai was saying, "He's our boy." There I was at Marco Island, this colorblind intern lecturing to the surgeons who wrote my textbooks.

Long hours, incredible stress, and the need for near-superhuman tolerance were all required to make it through a surgical internship. From the first day of being frightened and worried about making a mistake, and possibly harming a patient, to the last day, where I said to myself, "I actually know the right things to do to save a life in an emergency." It was truly an amazing journey.

The "dumb kid" notion was passing into oblivion. It was still amazing to me that my place in medicine was rising—but little did I know at the time that my colorblindness would come into play again—this time as an obstacle.

NEWS BRIEFS

DR. NEMIROFF AWARDED FOR MANUSCRIPT

Paul M. Nemiroff, M.D., a resident in the department of surgery, was awarded the 1981 Resident Fellow Award of the Society of Head and Neck Surgeons for his manuscript entitled "Extralaryngeal Divisions of the Recurrent Laryngeal Nerve: Surgical and Clinical Significance." The paper, which won first prize in the nationwide competition, was presented by Dr. Nemiroff at the Society's Annual Meeting on Marco Island, Florida, in April. □

Paul Nemiroff, M.D.

Cedars-Sinai News Brief—1981

7

GO GATORS

Approaching the end of my general surgery internship, I knew that I wanted to sub-specialize. Based on the influence of several professors, including Dr. Ward and Dr. Rice at UCLA, I decided ENT / Head & Neck surgery would be my area of advanced study.

In this field, you could have the best of both worlds—you could see patients in an office and build relationships (drawing on my PhD background in psychology), and you were still very much a surgeon, doing cases ranging from simple procedures like tonsillectomies (which aren't without risks), to voice box surgeries, on up to 15-hour facial reconstruction procedures due to cancer or accidents. Couple this with trauma cases involving the head or neck—it covered many areas of medicine and surgery that I knew would be exciting and challenging.

For my advanced resident surgical training, I interviewed at a number of institutions around the country, including Stanford, University of Texas, UCLA, and the University of Florida. My decision to go to University of Florida was based in part on my review of "The Green Book" of residency programs—a bible for med students, describing the various statistics of outpatient visits, cases that might be handled, and number of actual surgeries performed by the residents. At the time, it suggested that UCLA had about 20 residents, and around 26,000 outpatients per year. Florida saw about the same number of patients, but they had only eight surgical residents to handle the caseload. I reasoned that I might gain more experience at the University of Florida and would have a greater chance of doing more surgeries.

When I interviewed at Florida, the chairman of the program, Dr. Cassisi, personally picked me up at the airport, took me to his home, and seemed to be doing a full court press to recruit me. He was quite the charmer—a tall, slim Sicilian with silver hair. He knew I had many offers elsewhere. Cassisi said, "Paul, we really want you here."

After some thought, I decided to pursue a residency in Head & Neck surgery at the University of Florida. Once again, I loaded up my car and drove cross-country, this time from LA to Florida, with very high hopes, and a little bit of fear. I was embarking on at least four additional years of what was to be a grueling surgical training. Also, I hadn't done my homework on the exact location of the university—in Gainesville, in the center of Northern Florida, closer to Georgia than Miami—not the "white sand beaches and palm trees" vision I'd imagined.

Beyond The Normal Limits

Dr. Halstead is considered the "Father of American Surgical Residency Programs." An old "legend" describes how several residents approached him to ask him why they had to be on call every other night, versus general medicine residents who were on only every fourth night. His response was simple: "I know you residents want to be on every night, and not miss any of the fun, but you DO need to get some rest." However, Dr. Halstead, an incredibly famous surgeon of his day, had a dark secret—it turns out he was using cocaine to keep himself awake throughout most of his medical career, and spent years in a sanitarium trying to kick his habits. Some say after leaving the sanitarium—Halstead was never the same. It's only been relatively recently that this "dirty little secret" was formally announced to the world.

*"Today's medical education system has roots reaching back to the 1890s. Dr. William Stewart Halstead began the first formal surgical training program in the United States at Johns Hopkins Hospital in Baltimore, Maryland. He is widely considered one of the founders of the American residency training system. But in March 2005, the New England Journal of Medicine published an article profiling Halstead's addiction to cocaine throughout much of his medical career, suggesting that even at the system's beginnings, **residents pushed themselves beyond the normal limits of the human body.**"* [source: CNN]

The checkered legacy of Halstead was something many surgeons knew, and had quietly mentioned to those of us in training, but it was never openly discussed. The incredibly long hours were a rite of passage. I knew there was some insanity to it at the time, but this was my dream—being a surgeon. The bottom line was—you either performed, or you were out. Interestingly, today studies have shown that even though a surgeon may be very tired, it appears that no more mistakes are made than when there are much shorter hours with many "hand-offs" to other doctors throughout the day. It appears that more mistakes may be made during the transfer of information from one doctor to another.

All residencies, regardless of specialty, require dedication, desire, and effort, yet surgical residencies have always been more grueling than any other area of medicine. The "making of a surgeon" requires a physical strength and emotional toughness that is unique to the surgeon personality, both good and bad. Knowing this, I was undaunted at the long grueling hours at the University of Florida. It did, however, take a heavy toll on my personal life.

The Taskmaster

Although Dr. Cassisi was an outstanding surgeon, his training methods were severe—he directed his residents using an "iron fist" approach. Frequently, during an operation, when Dr. Cassisi would walk in to supervise, you immediately felt as if your IQ dropped 15 points. You were being "watched." All of it ultimately was about care for the patient, but there was zero tolerance for error, and perfection was the only outcome permitted.

Some of the cases could be as long as 13 hours in the operating room, demanding near superhuman levels of endurance. Once finished with the operation, you had to write post-operative orders, dictate the "op note" (i.e. operation report), of course speak with the family members, and then get ready for the next day's rounds. When going into the doctor's lounge to review my notes for the following day, I could slowly feel the fatigue consuming me as I collapsed into the chair. The day's adrenaline rush had long since passed.

Day after day, for four more years, the work continued. My supervisors thought I was bright, already having a PhD from Purdue University and training at UCLA and Cedars-Sinai, so there were extraordinarily high expectations of how technically competent I might be. In my mind, I was a big disappointment, I suspect, to Dr. Cassisi and another attending there, because I didn't pick up things on a "first pass." There's an old saying in surgery—"Watch one, do one, teach one"—meaning that you would watch a case, then actually do the case, then the next time around you would teach someone the case. For me, it was— "Watch about a dozen, have someone assist me with six of them, then I'd finally get it." It was never a "first pass" for me—but once I did "get it," watch out.

The X-Chrome Lens

A radical neck dissection involves removing tissue that may contain cancerous lymph nodes in the neck. One day while performing this procedure, I realized that I was definitely not seeing the same things as other people. Cassisi yelled at me, "Cut. Cut. Cut. G-- D---- It! Don't you see the different shades between the platisma (a thin pink muscle in the neck) and the other tissues, Nemiroff?"

The tissue planes contained shades of red and hues of blood

with minor subtleties. I thought to myself, "Oh no, I don't want to cause anybody harm because I'm colorblind." Maybe this was why it took me longer to learn procedures, because of the color variations in the various tissue planes.

I began researching color blindness and found an optometrist in Gainesville who introduced me to a red contact lens that he said might actually help me— the "X-Chrome Lens." The red lens blocks out red wavelengths, tricking the brain into perceiving or "seeing" different colors. When I put the lens on my right eye, it made it look bloodshot, however I started to improve on tests for color blindness, and thought I could actually see colors that I had never seen before.

Imagine a surgeon trying to overcome this obstacle of color blindness—keeping in mind the #1 rule of medicine: "First, do no harm." Prior to using this lens, I thought my career in surgery might be over. Suddenly, I could "see." Although being color blind had helped me back at Cedars-Sinai to identify nerves that split, or bifurcated, in the neck—and led to my becoming an expert thyroid surgeon—color blindness was clearly a mixed blessing.

The next day I went into the OR with the special lens. Everything was so vibrant—the subtle colors of the various tissue planes suddenly became more distinguishable, and my skill increased. Over time, I realized that I didn't have to always wear the lens, and I could see the important structures and tissues, perhaps because of other senses taking over. It was almost as if the X-Chrome Lens was the "training wheel" needed for a lifelong career in surgery.

Occasionally I would wear the X-Chrome Lens for fun, and

people started referring to it as my "Bionic Eye" or calling me "Dr. Red-Eye." In some instances, I could actually see things the average person with "normal" vision could not, and came to understand that what I once thought was a "label with negative connotations" might have some advantages.

This "perceptual difference" may be one of reasons I started to excel at certain types of Head & Neck surgery, especially thyroid surgery. The subtle shades of color in nerves seemed to glisten and jump out at me, thus I could avoid making cuts that could injure the patient.

On an emotional level, I felt like a deaf person hearing for the first time. I could see sunsets differently, and I could see the leaves changing colors in a way I hadn't experienced before. It was like being a kid again, experiencing things anew.

As I write this, I flashback to the early days of my color blindness, when my brother (who like me has the same "affliction") wanted to surprise my Mom on her birthday with a matching purse for her brown shoes. I was about 10, my brother around 16, and he had his driver's license. We climbed into the car and drove to May Company in the San Fernando Valley to find a purse. Using our paper route money, we bought her what we thought was a cool-looking brown purse—a perfect match. At the birthday party when my Mom opened our gift in front of all her friends, everybody laughed—because it was bright kelly green. My Mother refused to return the purse and proudly wore it with her non-matching shoes.

Double Secret Probation

Without warning one day Cassisi called all the residents into his office for a meeting. There had been a problem with a "work up" on a patient, and he was yelling at each one of us—finding fault with something we had done. When he got to me, he said he wasn't quite sure what I had done, but it must have been something—and if I wasn't careful, he would only let me operate on rats, not people. He was snidely referring to my recent award-winning research from an American Cancer Society grant involving wound healing—the fact that part of the study used rats as "guinea pigs."

Cassisi then said, "If you guys don't like the way I'm running things, you should put your beepers on the table and get out." Of course, no one moved, because it would have meant the end of their career. We all quietly left the room, feeling rattled.

Over the next few weeks, half of us were put on probation— for reasons that weren't entirely clear. We were told that if our performance didn't improve, or we didn't follow Cassisi's rules, we would be kicked out of the program. My life's dream felt like it was hanging by a thread. I was devastated and truly didn't know what I had done wrong.

Recalling the movie *Animal House* starring John Belushi (who had "passed through" Cedars-Sinai while I was there), I remarked to my other comrades that we had to behave, or Cassisi would put us on "Double Secret Probation," (a line from the movie) whatever that meant.

I knew that Cassisi had fired residents in the past, and being on probation, "double secret" or otherwise, was a serious matter. To cover my bases and develop a possible "exit strategy," I flew out to LA and quietly met with the head of USC's Program for Head & Neck surgery, Dr. Dale Rice. As mentioned, Dr. Rice had been one of my mentors at UCLA, but was now the head of this program, and he knew me well. He told me that if I wanted to transfer there, they would take me. The only catch was that he couldn't take me until the next year, which meant adding still another year of training. I thanked him and told him I would see how things worked out with Dr. Cassisi, and flew back to Florida the next day.

It seemed as if I couldn't do anything right to please two of the attending surgeons, Dr. Cassisi and Dr. Singleton, although I got along fine with the other attending surgeons. I remember shaking in the shower at 5 a.m. before making rounds, hot water running down my back, worrying about what abuse I might encounter that day from Cassisi or Singleton. This was a tough residency with frequent 100-hour workweeks. Sometimes it seemed unbearable, but I was determined to see it through.

Whitewall Syndrome

Back at Shands Hospital in Florida (known for being the birthplace of the drink Gatorade® among many other things— Go Gators), I began to gain more and more responsibility in the operating room. All surgical training, regardless of the specialty, demands that the resident assume greater responsibility and perform increasingly difficult procedures. On any given day, an attending surgeon like Cassisi, might have three ORs going at the same time, running between the rooms to supervise.

At some point in a surgeon's training, when you are expecting your attending surgeon or supervisor to be there, you turn around and realize that—"you're it." You may have encountered a problem, but there's no time to call for assistance or backup, because you have to make a decision right now. However no one is behind you except a blank white wall. In your head you're saying, "Someone call a real doctor." This is known among surgeons as "White Wall Syndrome."

Surgeons must be decisive—there's no time for group consensus, nor time for pondering the philosophies and potential outcomes of the future. You have to either "fish or cut bait," so to speak.

The Popcorn Can Incident

In Gainesville, Florida there were occasional "high rollers" who came to Shands Hospital at the medical center with a briefcase full of money to pay for their surgeries. One day a man in his 30s showed up in our clinic, complaining of hoarseness. He sounded like a croaking frog. I asked him typical questions while "working him up."

I asked him, "Do you drink?" He responded, "Only an occasional glass of wine."

"Do you smoke?" He answered, "No, I don't smoke tobacco."

When I examined his vocal cords, I saw an obvious fungating cancer, eventually confirmed on biopsy. The man said he had no health insurance, but would pay cash for any and all surgery needed. I said that I had nothing to do with the financial end, but he was determined to show me that he had the cash available for whatever was needed. He then proceeded to open a briefcase filled to the brim with stacks of $100 bills.

We explained that the type of surgery he needed to save his life would be quite extensive, including a possible laryngectomy, which is the removal of the voice box. As I was discussing the procedure with him, he then shared with me that, while he would never use tobacco, he did smoke "a little pot" once in a while. In his case, a "little pot" was 10-15 joints a day. I told him that marijuana is a potential carcinogen, much like tobacco, and is not without risks, especially at this level of use.

The surgery went well, he was discharged, and he always insisted on paying his bills in cash. However he didn't show up for his follow up appointments, and all attempts to reach him were unsuccessful. I often wondered whether he was OK and what happened to him.

One day a package arrived for me at the hospital clinic—a large popcorn tin can—the kind with dividers separating the flavors, like caramel, butter, natural, etc. On the top, I saw a note, which read: *"Thanks Doc for all your help. This is how I sometimes have some extra cash on hand. Enjoy."*

Peering inside, I saw what appeared to be a can full of cannabis—he was a dope dealer, I presumed. What the heck was he thinking, sending it here? I quickly turned the "pot-corn" over to the powers that be. Without naming names, one particular resident asked if I would like to take a "restroom break" before I turned it in. Enough said.

Gator Gas

On a more serious note, there was a day in Shands Hospital, when I held a 4 year-old child in my arms who couldn't breathe. I knew the kid's history well. His respiratory problems were due to growths on his vocal cords called laryngeal papillomas. We would have to use a "CO2 laser" (a cumbersome antique by today's standards) to "buzz off" the tumors so he could breathe.

There wasn't any time for paperwork, he was in our clinic dying. I grabbed him, and with his Mother running up stairs behind me, I ran into an OR telling them to get me a "trach" set, STAT. An anesthesiologist who happened to be there suggested that the patient get one "quick try" using something called "Gator Gas" before I cut a hole into the boy's neck [i.e. before I would have to do a tracheostomy].

The so-called Gator Gas (named because of the Florida's mascot—the Gators), was a mixture of helium and oxygen used at NASA to help reduce fire risks with astronauts. The helium, being lighter than oxygen, could "pull" the oxygen along with it more easily through obstructions, and thus into the lungs. At the time it was entirely experimental. Fortunately the anesthesiologist was very "slick" and no tracheostomy was required after all. The tumors were lasered off and the boy did well. Gator Gas, or Heli-Ox as it's now called, is now available routinely in many emergency rooms for treating certain emergency respiratory problems.

With All Due Respect

Sometimes you are made an offer that you have to "politely refuse." The source of this offer, in my case, was a well-dressed man (we'll call him "Vinnie") with a three-piece suit, an Italian last name, and two intimidating "bodyguards," who walked into my clinic at the VA hospital (part of the University of Florida teaching-medical system). As I recall, Vinnie had some early cancer on one of his vocal cords—we were able to remove the cancer and treat him successfully with a great outcome.

Vinnie would frequently say to me, "Eh Doc, eh Doc. I want you should have something [sic]." He'd then take out a $100 bill, shove it in my shirt pocket, pat me on the cheek, and say, "Kid— you done a good job, this is for you." I'd always hand it back and thank him, saying I couldn't accept the gift, but I appreciated the gesture. Then one day he insistently said, "Oh yes—you CAN accept it." I didn't argue.

Later Vinnie insisted I have lunch with him to discuss some "future opportunities with his organization," serving as one of their "in-house docs." Vinnie indicated he would build a special office for me with an operating room in South Florida. As an added bonus, he said, "Don't worry about ever getting sued, kid. As long as you're with 'our family' you won't have to worry about nothing."

My first thought, as naïve as I was: "Is he after drugs?" Later I realized that he just wanted me to do operations on his "associates" who might encounter an occasional gunshot wound or knifing, and maybe "forget" to report it to the police.

I told Dr. Cassisi about the situation, and being a Sicilian, he had heard of these types of situations being offered in the past. He said, "Stay away from these guys, or they will own you." I gingerly explained to Vinnie that I greatly appreciated his offer, and his "kindness and warmth as a human being," but since I was going into academic medicine, I had to decline—with all due respect. Fortunately, he was OK with this and wished me well. I haven't spoken with him since. As twisted as it sounds, for a moment or two, I'll think back to that day when Vinnie almost made me an offer I couldn't refuse. I can only imagine where that road may have led.

Blood On The Ceiling

While at Shands Hospital, we also covered the VA Hospital. One day while making rounds at the VA on cancer patients early in the morning, I suddenly heard a man yelling and a nurse screaming for a doctor to get there—STAT. A patient's main artery to the brain, the carotid artery, had ruptured, about a week after his surgery. This was known as a "carotid blow out," and was frequently deadly.

Blood from this man's neck had hit the ceiling and droplets were falling back down on him. I immediately placed my finger over the artery, and while holding pressure, called for the anesthesiologist to roll the patient into the operating room. The patient during this time was fully conscious. If I let my finger off the "dike," he would bleed to death in a matter of minutes. Prior to him being put to sleep for the procedure, he grabbed my other hand and looked at me with fear and terror in his eyes and said, "Please don't let me die, Doc."

We prepped the patient, slapped some betadine on his neck to quickly clean the area, and the anesthesiologist was able to put him to sleep. As the OR nurse quickly set up the instruments necessary for the procedure, I then proceeded to make the incisions and to dissect both above and below the "blowout point" of the carotid artery. The intent was to close up the hole in the large pipe that feeds the brain, and if I couldn't patch the hole, I might have to clamp the carotid artery to save his life.

However, stopping blood flow to the brain could cause a massive stroke. Like so many surgeons in the OR, you make decisions quickly, decisively, based on years of training and experience.

I began cracking out orders: "Hemostat. Metzs. Five-o Prolene sutures. Double-ball retractor"—all things needed to help control the bleeding. Using a Satinski Clamp, I was able to "over-sew the artery," a type of suture technique which pulls the artery together where the hole was, without having to clamp it shut and risk a stroke.

As I removed the clamp, I held my breath to see if it would hold. Much like testing a flat tire under water to see where the leak might be, I took a syringe of saline, squirted it over the area to see if there were any leaks. There weren't. He seemed OK and recovered from the surgery.

As I pulled off my gloves and my gown and took a deep breath of relief, realizing how close we were to losing him, I said my trademark line (to help relieve some stress): *Another day of saving lives—every day's a party.*

I wiped the blood from my mask and face and cleaned up. Then, I went to talk with the man's family and reassured them that he was OK for now. Next, I continued making my rounds, which were long delayed because of the emergency. The rooms at the time in the VA were ward rooms, with eight beds in a room. The man next to the gentleman who had the carotid artery blowout was scheduled for a simple septo-plasty—the straightening of a deviated piece of cartilage in the nose—a relatively straightforward procedure with relatively few risks.

However, the man was hovering underneath sheets, saying,

"Get me out of here—I don't want blood dripping from the ceiling with me, like that other guy." We tried to explain to him that his was a different procedure, and had nothing to do with the other guy's surgery. "Nothin' doing," he said. He checked out—never to be seen again.

A Common Thread

One of my patients at the VA was a former fighter pilot in WWII who claimed to have been the wingman for Chuck Yeager—the first man to break the sound barrier. My patient had cancer of his voicebox that had metastasized (spread to other areas in the body) and was "inoperable."

The statistics said he should die soon—yet somehow he beat all the odds and continued to live for many years. I wondered: "What is it about his immune system that allows him to survive, when others in his situation all died?" It was something that I would later come to understand with my own health situation. Could I theoretically boost my own immune system to fight my blood disorder using therapies that were not "standard of care?"

Although our situations were different, they still involved abnormal cells and cancer. After I was diagnosed with the malignancy (MDS), I began researching and thought back to this gentleman. *What common thread might there be between us? How might I extend my survival?*

The Slammer

Periodically senior residents at Shands Hospital would have the opportunity to operate and "fine tune" some of their skills at a maximum security penitentiary (aka "the slammer") north of Gainesville. Since these "felons" included rapists, murderers and pedophiles who had virtually no other access to surgical care, we were "it." It was a great training ground for residents. We learned *not* to look at the convicts' charts before surgery to see why they were in prison—to maintain our objectivity as best we could. While it was a dangerous environment, every time we operated on a prisoner the guards were close at hand.

While many convicts did legitimately need surgery because of broken jaws, broken noses, or broken faces from a fight, there was often "another reason" they volunteered for surgery—and that was to receive pain medications afterwards.

One day I was getting ready to operate on a prisoner—a huge, balding, six-foot-something, tattooed, Swastika-wearing, neo-Nazi type—to try to fix his broken face. As I was getting ready to give him a local injection of numbing medicine, he reached up and grabbed my throat and said menacingly, "Don't f--- up, doc, or I'll kill you."

Quickly I grabbed a scalpel and held it to his neck above the carotid artery and told him to let go. In what seemed like an instant, two guards with "Smokey the Bear" type hats and batons were upon him. "Step out of the room, doctor," they said. All I know is that I saw some batons flying, and this man's broken face became the least of his problems.

Double Secret Probation—Removed

As required by surgical residency programs, I took the annual Otolaryngology Head & Neck surgery exams. I knew I had done well, but had no idea that I scored highest in the country that year—in the 99th percentile. My feelings of being a "dumb kid" and fear of standardized tests evaporated—I couldn't believe it. Yet I remember one of the attendings, a good ol' boy, saying to me, "Nee-mer-roff, even though you think you walk on water now—you're still on probation."

Undaunted, I continued operating and conducting research work at Shands Hospital about how I could help damaged tissue heal faster. I applied for and received a highly coveted research grant from the American Cancer Society for my proposal. In essence, the study involved a way to improve wound healing after radiation using something called "hyperbaric oxygen therapy."

Hyperbaric oxygen (HBO) can help damaged tissues heal faster through a variety of ways—including increasing the oxygen levels to the tissues, helping killer white cells work more efficiently to kill bacteria, as well as reducing swelling of tissues. The University of Florida had a huge "HBO" unit, which was used as a decompression chamber for divers, and as a "back-up" unit, which potentially could be used to treat astronauts in the event of a decompression injury.

While making rounds one day, I asked if we could send a patient to the hyperbaric tank to see if it might help close the wounds on his neck—he had high dose radiation after his cancer surgery, and the wounds just wouldn't heal. Cassisi said, "Sure"—since although this man's cancer had been "cured," he was in such agony that he wished he were dead.

The patient received numerous "HBO" treatments and eventually healed up. It gave me pause—"Maybe there's something to this HBO stuff after all?" I became fascinated with it and pursued my own research with it. Since we were required to do research during our residency program, this was the perfect area for me—how to get tissue and wounds to heal faster—what supplements might help that weren't part of "traditional medicine" and what about this HBO stuff?

I designed a wound healing study using hyperbaric oxygen—the bottom line of the study is we found that "flaps" of tissue healed faster with the use of HBO. For my groundbreaking work on flap and hyperbaric oxygen and radiation, I received one of the top research awards for the year from the American Academy of Otolaryngology/Head & Neck Surgery. Even Cassisi said it was the best research he'd ever seen. Yet, I was still on "Double Secret Probation."

I was invited to present my work at our upcoming national meeting to hundreds of surgeons in Las Vegas. Dr. Cassisi was there with me, and I was one of "his boys" (as he put it) who received an American Cancer Society grant, gaining national recognition for cutting edge research, and then scoring highest in the country on the Head & Neck surgery exams. As he was about to begin the presentation, he put his arm around me at the podium and said, "Dr. Nemiroff is one of our best residents." Before beginning my speech, I leaned over to him, in front of the hundreds of attendees (cupping my hand over the microphone) and asked Dr. Cassisi, "Am I now off Double Secret Probation?" *I was.*

After this, my relationship with Cassisi improved markedly and he came to trust and believe in me as a competent, well-trained surgeon. The crowning event for me was when a patient was on the table and I made a decision to cancel the surgery.

Cassisi was tied up and couldn't be there in the beginning, but was furious when he learned that I had cancelled the surgery without first consulting him. It was one of those decisions you had to make right then and there—after reviewing the scans and scoping the patient (examining the patient while they are under anesthesia), I realized that this man's cancer was inoperable. We would only do the patient harm by trying to operate.

Cassisi immediately demanded I come to his office. He was furious and ranting. As I showed him the scans, and called the respected radiologist Dr. Tony Mancuso an expert and pioneer with reading MRI scans (another UCLA prof gone to Florida), Cassisi turned to me and said, "You're right, we couldn't have operated on this man and been successful."

By the look in his eye, and a small smirk on his face, and a final nod, I knew I had "arrived." This was confirmed a day later, when making rounds, he turned to me in front of all the other residents and said, "Dr. Nemiroff, I'd like your opinion and input on this upcoming case of mine. How would you proceed?"

We all learned to be good surgeons under Cassisi's and others' mentoring. Dr. James Garlington was one of my greatest mentors there, and has become a lifelong friend. (More about Jim later.) The sheer volume of cases I did or assisted in, about 2500, gave me an amazing foundation.

One of Cassisi's sayings was: "Nemiroff, I can teach a monkey how to tie a knot, and I can teach somebody how to cut skin, but a real surgeon knows how to stay out of trouble—and if he gets into trouble, he knows how to get out."

Cassisi also said, "Nemiroff, as bright as you are, you still need a 'gimmick' to be successful." The word "gimmick" sounded cheap to me, and I asked him what he meant. He said, "All people need gimmicks—maybe your wound healing and hyperbaric research could be yours."

This gave me pause—I thought of all the patients who had undergone radiation and chemo treatments whose wounds wouldn't heal properly. Some had been treated with this stuff called "HBO"—not Cinemax® or Showtime®— but hyperbaric oxygen—an adjunctive medical treatment used to help heal damaged tissue, which has many other uses as well. This, in fact, became one of my areas of expertise.

In the years to come, I would continue research on hyperbaric oxygen, publish many articles, and lecture all over the country, including TV interviews, and was viewed by many as an expert on the subject. It was the first time I truly realized how powerful the media could be to spread a message about medical advances.

8

LAND OF LINCOLN

By the time I finished my residency at the University of Florida, my "gimmick"—hyperbaric oxygen—as well as being an award-winning head and neck surgeon, had made something of a name for me, though many at the time thought these strange new HBO chambers to be a bit of "witchcraft." That thinking would eventually change.

For me, the question became where to go next. I loved doing research—having published many articles, I felt like my true calling was teaching and academic medicine. It had been a long ride since high school, with nearly 18 years of additional education, including college, Masters, PhD, MD, general surgery training, ENT and Head & Neck surgery training. Of course, there was a short hiatus after my PhD when I was in the "real world" as the Director of Staff Development at Kaiser Permanente hospitals, and I also always had additional jobs throughout most of my education.

I had many opportunities to go into private practice, as well as academics. I interviewed at Johns Hopkins, Stanford, and others, but I was asked, as a courtesy by Dr. Cassisi and another

attending at Florida, to interview in Springfield, Illinois
(Abraham Lincoln's birthplace)—at Southern Illinois University
(SIU). They were seeking a new assistant professor in the
department of surgery specializing in head & neck. While SIU
hadn't previously been on my radar, at all, I went for an
interview.

My first impression of Springfield, Illinois was not particularly
positive. It was a freezing cold wintry day with snow on the
ground. I was constantly shocked by every doorknob in the hotel
and elsewhere, and there was no sun—I know, I know, how
superficial. This wasn't a place in which I was particularly excited
about living. However, the people I met were nice and cordial.
They also made a generous offer, asking me what I wanted and
needed to build a research program. In fact, they went to far as
to ask me to write a "wish list" for research needs, with virtually
no apparent limit on the budget.

Knowing my interest in hyperbaric medicine and wound care,
they said they would finance and help me start the first center of
its kind at the university and in the entire southern part of the
state. None of the other universities had "stepped up to the
plate" to allow me to do this level of research. In addition to
doing research, I would be teaching and continuing my surgical
practice. It was an opportunity second to none at the time. After
several more visits and discussions, I accepted the offer and
headed to the "Land of Lincoln."

Upon arriving in Springfield, my wife at the time and I began
looking for a place to live. I had married during my residency in
Florida. There was a house for lease about 15 miles away from
the hospital. It was a spectacular home with three stories that

reminded me of some I'd seen in California with big windows and tremendous openness. A problem was that it was in the middle of cornfields, far away from civilization. However, the rent was so reasonable, I couldn't resist.

Little did I know that the propane heating bill would cost a fortune. Coupled with the well-water system, with some sort of reverse filtration that didn't always work—well, it was quite an experience. The water there never tasted right, and the white haze that appeared every time the faucet was opened made me think it was less than safe. Obviously, the bottled water bill added to the expense.

One night, when driving back from the hospital, I witnessed the worst lightening storm of my life. Intimidating as the storms were, I'd never witnessed anything quite so spectacular, with the exception of that Arctic moon when I was in Alaska. Lightning bolts crashed all around me in the cornfields as I drove to my house.

Only a day before, my Mom had come for a visit, and was trapped in the home with no power. When I got back to the house that night, she was hovered around some flashlights in the middle of the room. All these things caused me to think—did I really want to live here for the rest of my life?

Hyperbarics

The real excitement for me was the grand opening of the Hyperbaric Center where I continued doing research on wound care. There was a grand gala for the opening—news media and all. It was still a very controversial area of research in medicine and plenty of "naysayers" claimed I was practicing "witchcraft." Why would a respected surgeon doing cancer research become the developer and medical director of something that was "so out there?" My reason was simple—it worked.

With the center open, I continued doing my research on wound healing and publishing many articles. Soon I was lecturing all over the country as an invited speaker and expert on wound care and hyperbaric medicine. I was also teaching surgical residents how to operate on cancer cases, and had a full clinic of patients on a regular basis—it didn't leave much time for any personal life.

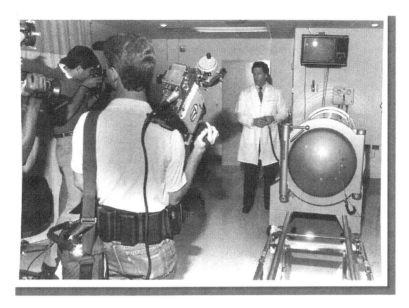

TV news media covering opening of Hyperbaric Center

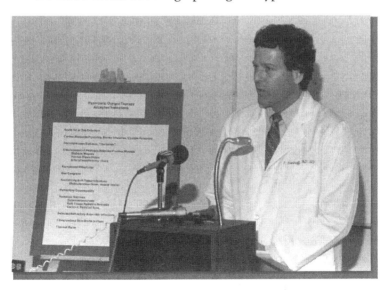

Delivering a presentation about Hyperbaric Oxygen Therapy

Heading To Rocket City

Although I wasn't there very long, SIU allowed me to do research, continue operating, and gave me an opportunity to build my reputation in hyperbaric medicine and wound care. I was now being courted even more heavily in the private sector.

Even though, for the first time in my life, I was making more than "minimum wage" as a surgeon, all the educational debt I had accrued was not being covered by my income—it just didn't go very far. For this reason (and others, including freezing cold weather), I decided it was time to make a move.

While at SIU, I was contacted frequently by headhunters, some offering very good opportunities at academic centers or private practice, but always declined. That changed when a former mentor and dear friend of mine from Florida, Dr. Jim Garlington, contacted me about a unique opportunity in Huntsville, Alabama. Jim had been the chairman of the Head & Neck Surgery Department at the University of Florida (Jacksonville) at the time.

Years before, Jim and I had talked about starting a practice together, or working in academic medicine. Jim is one of the finest people I know—honest, ethical, loyal and a great mentor. He convinced me to rendezvous in Huntsville and check out some exciting options. Despite my inaccurate preconceptions about Alabama, I agreed to meet him there. I soon learned that Huntsville was the birthplace of our Space Program—the International Space Station was being built there, and the rockets that put our astronauts into space, and eventually on the moon, were developed there.

After meeting with an administrator at one of the hospitals in

Huntsville, we realized this was not the opportunity we had hoped for. Jim and I had a few hours to kill before going back to the airport to return to our respective homes, so we decided to drop in at one of the other hospitals there—Humana.

As luck would have it, they were looking for someone to start a wound care and hyperbaric center. They explained that Huntsville was also in need of Head & Neck surgeons. This would become the start of a thirteen-year stretch where I developed and became medical director of my next wound care center and hyperbaric facility, and built a thriving surgical practice.

February 26, 1988   The State Journal-Register   Springfield, Illinois

SIU professor to head new institute

Dr. Paul Nemiroff, assistant professor at Southern Illinois University School of Medicine, is moving to head a new institute for hyperbaric research in Huntsville, Ala.

Nemiroff will leave his Springfield position March 11 and will begin work in Huntsville in April.

Hyperbaric medicine uses pressure chambers in which patients breathe pure oxygen at high pressures.

Nemiroff has been director of a hyperbaric medicine program at Memorial Medical Center, where a chamber has been in operation since last May under the joint sponsorship of the school of medicine and the hospital. It is used to treat infections and to cleanse the systems of patients suffering from carbon monoxide or cyanide poisoning.

Nemiroff said the Huntsville research program is under the joint sponsorship of the U.S. Air Force, the National Aeronautics and Space Administration and the Humana Hospi-

tal in Huntsville. A major university also will take part in the program.

A major subject of research will be development of a hyperbaric chamber for the proposed space station.

Boeing, an aircraft manufacturer and a participant in space station development, has its space station activities headquartered in Huntsville, Nemiroff said.

Hyperbaric or pressure chambers have been used for many years to return deep sea divers to normal air pressure after being exposed to the high pressures that exist in deep waters. A chamber could perform the same function for space station residents, only in reverse. In addition, the chamber could be used for medical treatment, Nemiroff said.

Nemiroff, a head and neck surgeon and specialist in diseases of the ears, nose and throat, expects to continue to practice medicine as well as head the research institute.

Quarters for the institute are under construction in Huntsville, he said.

[reprinted with the permission of The State Journal Register—Springfield, Illinois—February 26ᵗʰ, 1988]

9

ROCKET CITY

After years in academia and the operating room, I was ready to "do my own thing" and open up my own hyperbaric center and private medical and surgical practice. I would still keep my contacts in academia by becoming a clinical associate professor of surgery at Vanderbilt University.

Prior to getting to Huntsville there were many ups and downs in trying to set up the practice and the hyperbaric center. My buddy Dr. Jim Garlington, a surgeon and former malpractice lawyer (he was on the side of the docs), started putting together various business plans. We decided to go into practice together in Huntsville and had many meetings with the "legal beagles" of Humana Hospital (later renamed to Huntsville Hospital East). Various obstacles presented by the attorneys made it seem like all was lost and no arrangement could be made.

I awakened at 4 a.m. one morning with a flash of "brilliance" and called one of the key guys (an administrator) at Humana. I told him my new idea on a way to set up a hyperbaric center—and how it would be a "win" for all parties—it would especially benefit patients of North Alabama, since they didn't have a unit there, and this would be the first one of its kind.

I wanted to share the good news with Jim Garlington, but he'd just left for a month in Europe with his wife Peg—emails and cell phones weren't an option back then. The best-laid plans waited a month until his return.

Jim and I, the Humana administrator, and many other legal beagles, signed many documents, and I felt like I was signing my life away for this new opportunity. This, coupled with work I had planned to do at the University and with NASA, made for very exciting times.

When things finally settled down, Jim and I rented some space in a dingy little office while we waited to open our practice in a new building connected to the hospital. A couple days before our grand opening, the loan we were supposed to receive from the bank fell through, because the person who made the loan—well, made promises he couldn't keep. What would we do?

We "pounded the streets" in a frenetic attempt to secure crucial startup funds. One bank finally took a chance and loaned us the money to move forward—it was a big risk for all involved.

The night before we opened our practice, we scrambled to get things in order—vacuuming the floor (the cleaning crew hadn't shown up yet), getting chart racks together, making preparations, and hoping for a busy first day. In fact, my first day I had all of one patient. He happened to be the mayor from a nearby city who said he was here to see what the "new kid" on the block had to offer him for his problem. Aside from his visit, the office was fairly quiet, so I read a lot of journals. However, this mayor apparently started to put the word out that we "were OK," and referrals gradually started to come.

Building the practice required that Jim and I be on call every other night. We worked 90-hour weeks, and literally opened boxes of equipment for the development of the hyperbaric facility. It seemed as if there was one obstacle after another in getting this facility open.

First, an Alabama Fire Marshall said, "If there's an explosion, these walls aren't thick enough" ("Oh great," I thought). Just as this issue was resolved, another problem arose. The hyperbaric chambers used so much oxygen that the first time we turned it on, alarms and sirens went off all over the hospital. We figured out it was our HBO tank "stealing" oxygen from other places. This problem was resolved with our own dedicated "oxygen pot" in-house.

Soon after this, a very negative article came out about HBO. Someone, obviously not a fan of the therapy, posted copies of the article all over the doctor's lounges in all the hospitals of the city. One doctor said to me, "You have such a good name as a surgeon—why would you mess around with this hyperbaric stuff, when it seems so controversial, almost like witchcraft?" "Here we go again," I thought.

Meeting resistance is nothing new to innovators, especially in medicine. Fleming, who discovered penicillin, was met with skepticism. Doctors who argued that stomach ulcers were in large course caused by bacteria were ridiculed and accused of being "quacks," although they were later vindicated. Despite the resistance, I had done my own basic research, and being a practicing surgeon, I knew that this therapy could be used to help treat problem wounds and help tissue heal faster, in some cases. But in some peoples' minds—it was "pushing the envelope."

There was a fair amount of ridicule I took early on from less informed docs. I believe I was a contradiction for some of the people there. It only made me more determined to educate others about the value of hyperbaric medicine. Unfortunately, sometimes we physicians are resistant to change, and new ways of treating diseases are viewed as suspect, as they should be—until decent research is done.

In medicine, the "gold standard" for research is a "double-blind randomized placebo-controlled study." However, many treatments that we take for granted today never went through this rigor, but provided obvious beneficial effects for the patient—including penicillin, radiation treatments, and others. Undaunted, my interest in HBO as well as other complementary medicine approaches continued.

As a scientist, I believe in controlled studies and this "gold standard" as being the ideal. However, sometimes *simple* observations are a good place to start. Over time, more and more studies showed the value of HBO treatment for helping with specific diseases.

Day after day, week after week, I would try to educate small groups of physicians and nurses in Huntsville and surrounding areas about the value of this treatment—that it wasn't quackery, wasn't bad treatment, it had a place. Over time, doctors who were "naysayers" eventually saw the value and utility of this potentially life-saving treatment.

One that comes to mind was a horrific case of flesh-eating bacteria, literally eating away a man's skin and muscle tissue. Near death, he was finally referred for treatment. I am convinced that HBO, coupled with surgery and antibiotics, saved the man's life. This notable case raised our profile and soon the HBO chamber was running 24/7. Another chamber was installed over time, and more and more people, with various medical problems were being treated and helped.

We publicized the grand opening of the hyperbaric facility, and a presentation was to be held at the Space and Rocket Center in Huntsville. Next-door was one of the original rockets that launched American astronauts into space. Hundreds attended. One of the presenters was one of the doctors who took care of the little girl who had fallen in a well the year before—"Baby Jessica" McClure. Hyperbaric oxygen was credited with contributing to her foot not having to be amputated. After this, referrals increased even more so, and the unit continued to grow and expand and be an accepted additional treatment for many diseases.

Oxygen treatment saved Jessica's foot: 3A

Huntsville Times

Saturday, July 16, 1988   Price 25 Cents

The Huntsville Times, Saturday, July 16, 1988   3A

Jessica McClure's doctor says HBO saved her foot

By DAVID HOLDEN
Times Staff Writer

Dr. Charles Younger said hyperbaric oxygen (HBO) played a vital role in saving the foot of Jessica McClure, the little girl who spent more than two days trapped in a well in Texas last year.

"In my opinion, the hyperbaric oxygen treatments bought us the time that was necessary to save this little girl's foot," the Midland, Texas, orthopedic surgeon said during a news conference Friday in the new Hyperbaric Medicine Unit at Humana Hospital.

The toddler injured her foot while trapped in a well for 58 hours last October. Traditional treatments along with HBO were used to save her foot and return her to a normal life, Younger said.

"We treated her with standard medical care, including standard surgical procedures, standard antibiotic treatments and standard nutitional support," he said. "But, I think hyperbaric oxygen is what put us over the top to save this young girl's leg."

During hyperbaric oxygen treatments, patients are placed inside a decompression chamber where oxygen above normal atmospheric pressure enriches the oxygen in their blood. The technique was originally used to treat scuba divers who suffered from decompression sickness (the bends.)

Younger said he was not an expert in hyperbaric medicine, but he could see from the beginning

that HBO treatments were promising in this case.

"We put her in the tank within an hour after she hit the emergency room," he said. "We would put her in the chamber with her toes purple and in 15 to 20 minutes her toes would be nice and pink. They would remain nice and pink for three to four hours.

"We would repeat this three times a day during the first 10 days when the circulatory status and the viability status of her foot was in real question. It was a great feeling of security to see pink toes three hours a day as opposed to purple toes."

According to Younger the prognosis for little Jessica could hardly be better, even though she lost the fifth toe and 15 percent of the big toe on her injured foot.

"There is some scaring from the surgery, but circulation, feeling and functions are normal.

"She is doing very well," he said. "I saw her a couple of days ago. She can walk on her toes, she can run, jump and kick."

Younger said he used HBO because it could decrease swelling they knew was coming.

"The night she came in the foot was very compressed and flat from having pressure on it inside the small diameter of the well where her foot was up against her body," he said. "Although, she didn't have swelling in her foot, we knew it was going to swell. It had been shown the hyperbaric oxygen treatment can decrease swelling."

During the first 10 days, Jessica received HBO treatments for 90

minutes three times a day, Younger said. For the next 25 days, treatments were cut back to two per day.

"She is out of the hospital now and no longer requires treatments," he said.

The successful use of HBO in this case will probably give the technique more credibility and more acceptance in the scientific community in the future, Younger said.

"It was not accepted early on because people were asking it to do things it cannot do," he said. "I think now there is increasing evidence that it helps many, many, many conditions. I think the hype and publicity surrounding this case did a whole lot to legitimatize hyperbaric medicine. It worked."

Dr. Paul Nemiroff, director of hyperbaric medicine at Humana and a consultant to the U.S. Surgeon General on hyperbaric medicine, says safeguards have been taken to avoid past abuses of HBO.

"I think the hay day of HBO with respect to inappropriate uses is over," he said. "I'm on a board that reviews the abuses of HBO on a national level. Currently, there a approximately a dozen indications and they are updated every few years by the Undersea Medical Society, which basically governs the appropriate uses of HBO.

"I think most physicians in the country now, as they become more knowledgeable, know when HBO is useful and when it isn't. And if they don't know, they typically have experts in the field to contact."

The other patient to put HBO on the map in Huntsville was a retired U.S. congressman whose family brought him to us. He was an older gentleman on the verge of suicide because of the pain he was experiencing after his treatment for laryngeal and throat cancer. He had these large ulcers on his throat that refused to heal. His doctors thought it was because he had recurrent cancer, but my research led me to believe it was due to radiation necrosis—a condition that occurs when wounds resulting from radiation do not heal, because of lack of oxygen. He was drinking and on narcotics because he couldn't stand the pain.

I took him to the OR with the other surgeon who had treated him and checked out his throat. We took a scraping from one of his ulcers and did a biopsy but we couldn't find any cancer.

I thought I could fix this guy. "Congressman," I said, "I don't think you have recurrent cancer. Give me one month. If you can hang in there, I think we can get this pain down." We stuck him in the chamber and not much happened in the first couple of weeks—but the third week he said, "I don't know if I'm imagining this, but my pain is going down."

He walked out of that place alive and well, and lived for years after that—he never had recurrent cancer. It was radiation necrosis—which healed with use of HBO, nutritional supplements, and a good diet. After that, the word got out. The HBO unit took off, as well as our surgical practice, and culminated with receiving an honor from the State of Alabama— I was presented with a plaque for "Humanitarian Of The Year" for donating my time and skills to operate on war refugees from Bosnia.

The Twister

I mentioned before that the lightning storms in Springfield, Illinois were the most frightening thing I had seen since the fires of Alaska. I take it back—neither compared to the day the legendary F-4 Tornado hit Huntsville, Alabama, on November 15th, 1989.

I had finished surgery early and began making rounds on patients. One family physician had asked that I meet him in one of his patient's rooms at 4 p.m. to consult about the patient's problems. I went to the room and introduced myself to the patient. I then waited and waited, but the family doctor didn't arrive. Just about that time, the overhead loudspeaker in the hospital asked all surgeons to report to the ER. There had been some form of catastrophe and patients were being brought in left and right.

The massive F4 tornado had hit a local mall, and they expected hundreds of casualties. Ambulance after ambulance brought in everything from scratches and cuts to some horrific sights. I spent the next 24 hours in the hospital seeing patients and operating. The influx was so overwhelming that patients began to be triaged. Triage is a medical term which describes choosing between helping three types of patients, when you really can only immediately help one:

- **Patient A**—even if you treat him, will probably die.

- **Patient B**—will probably be ok and make it for a while, even if you don't treat him.

- **Patient C**—is the critical one, who unless you turn your attention to him right now, will die. It's never easy—but you have to pick Patient C.

One lady had her elbow crushed from debris, her abdomen ripped open, and what appeared to be a portion of a 2x4 smashed through her mandible and face. Mrs. B was rushed to the OR, and two other surgeons and I began to work on her. A general surgeon began repairing her belly wounds. An orthopedic surgeon worked on her elbow, and as a Head & Neck surgeon, I started to remove splinters from her face and tried to reconstruct her mandible and upper jaw into some semblance of order. Mrs. B. survived, but developed a blood infection and was in and out of consciousness for days. When she awakened, her hope was to see her grandkids on Christmas. She did. The next day her sepsis overwhelmed her and she died on December 26th.

The tornado wrought tremendous destruction. The entire shopping mall was leveled, looking like something out of WWII. Although there were nearly 500 casualties and about 25 deaths that day, it's amazing that more people weren't killed.

A small school, Jones Valley Elementary, was completely destroyed down to timber. Some children were there, and an after-hours worker gathered the kids and hid them under a stairwell. Everything was destroyed except for the one stairwell and none of the kids were seriously hurt—a miracle. A book from the Jones Valley library was later reportedly found 75 miles away. I drove by the mall and there was nothing left. Cars were piled up like toys on top of telephone poles dangling 100 feet above the ground in a weird balancing act.

The family doctor who'd been late for the consultation earlier that day had a "legitimate excuse." He was one of the casualties who had a portion of his arm severed off during the tornado. He did well over time with his prosthetic arm. I felt guilty that I'd ever doubted his punctuality.

At the time of this tragedy, part of me went into autopilot without emotion. After two days of essentially no sleep, driving home exhausted, I felt like maybe I had made some difference. I had been trained for situations like these. There was no worry about which insurance forms to fill out, or which HMO to call for approval. It was simply helping patients in need, in a desperate situation. You do your best during a time of tragedy.

Night From Hell

As an ENT and Head & Neck surgeon, you see a lot of nosebleeds. There are minor ones, and then there are the "real humdingers" that can be life-threatening. A full moon lit the sky, a beautiful sight—but for me it became "the night from hell," as I call it. I had been at several different hospitals that night packing and cauterizing noses from one cause or another, as well as patching people up from car accidents.

It was now 3 a.m.—I hadn't slept since the day before, and I finally drove home, pulled in the garage, and opened the door— when my beeper went off. Back to the hospital, a man had blood pouring through his nose like a faucet, and they couldn't stop it. "Get back here now," screamed the ER doc.

As I walked into the treatment room, the ER doc and a nurse were trying to help the young man with blood pouring out of his nose and mouth. He was very calm and nonchalant about the situation, saying, "Doc, I have a couple of questions before we get started."

He was used to having nosebleeds, because of his bleeding disorder, and it wasn't a big deal to him. He was more concerned about me—and wanted to know if I had any heart conditions. With blood dripping out of his mouth and nose, he explained that a doctor who treated him two weeks before in that ER had "dropped dead" of a heart attack. Fortunately, the doctor was revived with paddles. However, this patient didn't want to be the cause of any more heart attacks. I laughed and said, "No heart problems that I know of, I'm in great health. Let's get you taken care of."

Blood In Your Shoes

Another night from hell happened on a full moon—not that I'm superstitious. Most of the time, things go perfectly well after tonsillectomies, but every once in a while you get "a bleeder." I was on call and got a page that a young girl who had been operated on by another surgeon was about a week out from her surgery, and she was spitting out massive amounts of blood. As I flew back to the hospital in my BMW, I was calling the OR and the anesthesiologist telling them to get ready immediately.

I saw the kid in the ER—a cute little seven-year old redhead who was spewing out copious amounts of bright red blood, meaning that this was not "old" blood from her stomach, but rather that there was an active "bleeder" somewhere in her throat. The anesthesiologist and I spoke with the family quickly as we were rushing to prep her for surgery. With fear and terror, the father, an imposing six foot three guy, probably close to 300 pounds, threatened the anesthesiologist and me, saying, "If anything happens to my baby, I'll kill you."

The anesthesiologist very calmly turned and went up to the mom and dad and said, "I have a daughter about the same age. I will treat her like she's my own daughter, that I can assure you." The parents seemed somewhat relieved. It was only later that I learned these same parents had lost another child during a "routine surgical procedure" not long before. Not yet being a father, I couldn't understand the depths of the passion of this man for his daughter. It was only a couple years later when first my daughter Nicole and then Rachael came into the world, that I could begin to understand that bond.

Once in the OR, we prepped the little girl and got the appropriate equipment ready to try to stop the bleeding. We also had a "trach" set opened, just in case we couldn't get a breathing tube into her lungs. Suddenly, a massive amount of blood started to pour out of her mouth, nose, and even through her eyes—not a good situation. As I packed her throat, I took a deep breath and asked for some divine intervention.

I noted that blood was dripping onto my shoe covers and into my shoes. In my head, I recalled the old insensitive surgeon joke: *"You have nothing to worry about when's there bleeding during a case— until you have blood in your shoes."* There was blood in my shoes. I was worried.

Finally suctioning away the blood, I found the culprit and clamped a pencil-sized artery at the base of one of the tonsil beds, and "tied it off." I had feared, at one point, that perhaps her carotid artery had been damaged. I held by breath as she was awaked—and realized that all was well. No more bleeding and the little girl did fine.

Gunshot Wound

As a surgeon you sometimes have to put your real feelings on hold for a while—especially when there's an emergency. It's walking a line between being an "SOB" and not caring, and yet not taking all of your feelings home with you, or "feeling" all your emotions at a certain period of time. I'd learned this lesson earlier when working on convicts in a prison while in residency.

One night, when a guy was brought in and I was STAT paged to the ER, it took all my will to contain my real feelings. A young woman had been brutally beaten and raped by an "intruder." She had the "wherewithal" to pull a small .22 caliber from her bedside to finally try to get the guy to leave—and when he repeatedly smashed her face with his massive fists, she shot him in the forehead. The bullet entered and passed through his frontal sinuses and lodged near his pituitary in his brain.

I was the one on call and had the task of removing the bullet from this "person." First—being threatened by his family that if I made any mistakes on their "perfect" son, I would be sued. Then—spending numerous hours under a microscope carefully removing all the fragments I could. He survived and is hopefully still spending time in prison somewhere.

The police commentary was less-than politically correct: "Too bad you have to waste your time on this guy doc—she should have used a larger caliber." The girl who was raped and beaten did eventually recover, at least physically. Psychological scars can run deep and require great courage to overcome.

Fatherhood

A few years into my experience at Huntsville, I was at long last living my dream. I was wearing many hats, including medical director, surgeon, and also a Clinical Associate Professor of Surgery at Vanderbilt University. Life was good and very full.

My wife and I decided to start a family, and we had two kids, Nicole and Rachael. I delivered both of my kids, although a "real doctor"—OB/GYN—was also in the room. These were two of the most exciting moments in my life—I came to understand the depth of love one can have for their child—I wanted to protect them, help them grow, and achieve their dreams.

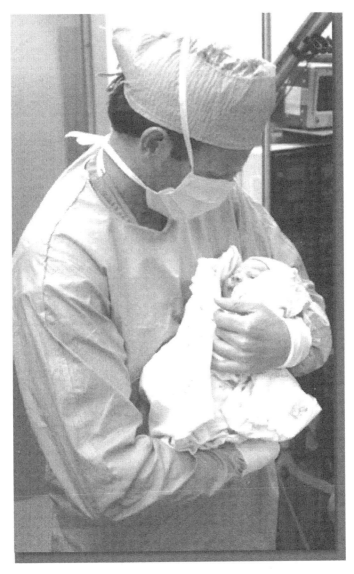

Dad holding daughter Nicole Nemiroff—June 28th, 1990

Dad with daughters Nicole and Rachael

Overall things were going well professionally. I had some money for the first time in my life. My school loans were finally paid off. I felt respected in the community. Grateful patients were constantly sending me cards and gifts. A little girl I treated brought me a teddy bear with a surgical mask. Another patient bought me a "star"—somewhere in the galaxy there's a star donated to me. I was in great shape, running, exercising and running marathons—my goal was to run a marathon in every state. I'd already done about a dozen, including the Boston 100th.

In November 1998, I received the news that I was selected winner of the Renaissance Runner of the Year by *Runner's World Magazine* and *Renaissance Hotels*. One night, while waiting for the results of a CAT scan on one of my patients, I wrote an essay in response to their question—simply: *"Why do you run?"* I received the award exactly one year before I was diagnosed with MDS, making the last sentence of my award-winning essay eerily prophetic:

"Why I Run: Running after completing a long cancer surgical case allows me to let go and truly appreciate being alive. While on a daily run, and especially when completing a marathon, I fully appreciate the mere fact that I am physically able to do this—many others, due to genetic defects, trauma, or cancer, have this gift taken from them. So just for today, I run, because I can."

PROFILE: RENAISSANCE® RUNNER
Paul Michael Nemiroff, Ph.D., M.D.
Residence: Huntsville, Alabama
Occupation: Head & Neck Surgeon,
North Alabama E.N.T. Associates, P.C.
Father of 2 daughters

*"Running after completing a long cancer surgical case allows
me to 'let go' and truly appreciate being alive."*

Achievements & Interests:
●My two daughters, Nicole and Rachel

●Finishing the 100th Boston Marathon in 1996

●Playing guitar, singing, and maybe beginning a rock-n-roll band

●Recipient of more than a dozen national awards for research

●Outstanding Humanitarian Award for surgery on Bosnian refugees

●Learning more about spirituality - my own and others

●Published and presented over 100 articles and papers

●Outstanding Teacher of the Year Award at Purdue University while
completing Ph.D.

Running Goal: Run a marathon in every state - 11 completed to date
Personal Goal: Peace of mind and personal serenity

Runner's World Magazine—1998

Paul M. Nemiroff, Ph.D., M.D.
Pittsburgh Marathon
Finisher
26.2 Miles
May 3rd, 1998

The second to the last of 13 marathons I ran

White Out

The UCLA Medical Alumni Society in Los Angeles invited me to attend a black tie affair at Fox Studios, hosted by numerous celebrities. It sounded like a fun event, supported charity, and they hoped I would come as an "invited special guest."

A few days before, I had developed a cough and started to get a low-grade fever. Of course, having worked insane hours and fighting through fatigue, I continued showing up to work and not thinking much about it, other than it might be the start of the flu. I was supposed to leave on Wednesday night for the event for Saturday, and decided maybe I'll be better the next day. This went on for a couple of days. I kept coughing and felt as if I were burning up. But I was in total denial about what might be going on, and continued to reschedule different flights, thinking that I would magically get better in 24 hours.

Finally on Friday morning, I was so sick that I couldn't get out of bed, and decided to go to the ER. I started to cough up some blood, and my fever hit 104 degrees. Some X-rays showed that one of my lungs was completely "whited-out," (meaning swelling and fluid) and the other lung was also involved. Doctors there were amazed that I was still able to walk. Because of my running marathons and being in great shape at the time, I was able to still marginally function. Nevertheless, they immediately admitted me to the hospital. They started running all sorts of tests, and realized that I had a very dangerous type of pneumonia called "Pneumococcus." This is the kind of pneumonia that can kill you quickly.

They ran many tests—ruling out HIV, hepatitis, and everything else, and weren't quite sure why I had gotten this. They asked many questions: "Were you around anyone recently with anything contagious?" I did recall that I had "trached" a patient emergently a week or so before in the ER and he had spewed all sorts of "stuff" over me—I learned later that he died of pneumococcal pneumonia—that was probably the connection.

The only thing on some of the tests on me that was a little disturbing was a low white blood cell count. White blood cells fight infection, and usually, when someone has this type of infection, their white cell count increases dramatically. Mine didn't. Later, I would learn that this low white blood cell count was the start of something even more ominous.

My fever continued to rise, and may have hit 105. Fortunately, with the right antibiotics I eventually recovered, but was left incredibly weak for months. For a long time after this, I felt some tingling in my hands and fingertips, and wondered if some of the circuitry in my brain had been damaged. I seemed to get hot and cold and didn't have great temperature regulation in my fingertips—not good for a surgeon.

Suddenly, a guy who had been in great shape and running marathons was, in the course of few days, reduced to such weakness that I couldn't walk across a room without being out of breath. People were shocked at my appearance because I was so "wasted looking."

Although I recovered over the weeks and months that followed, I noted that not only was I getting sick more often, but my running times continued to get worse. I tried to get more rest and cut way back on my exercise—mainly because I didn't have the energy to run 1 mile, let alone 26, but continued to have tremendous waves of fatigue and horrible night sweats. Suddenly, I felt as if I were 100 years old and struggled to get through each day.

10

FREQUENT FLYER

The strains of the demanding practice, the illness, as well as many other issues, caused the eventual ending of my marriage. When my ex-wife and I separated, it was more of a whimper than a bang, with both of us agreeing that it just wasn't working out. We were divorced in March of 1999. She remained in Huntsville with my daughters for a while—they would stay with me every Tuesday night and every other weekend. I'd also see them at other times during the week, if only to go to a t-ball or soccer game they were in. Things seemed to be okay—I was maintaining a good relationship with my kids.

A few months later, on June 17th, 1999, Father's Day, a shock wave hit. My ex-wife informed me during a phone call from New Castle, Pennsylvania, where she had taken the children for a "supposed" couple of week summer visit with her family, that she and the girls would not ever be returning to Huntsville. She also indicated there was nothing I could do about it. I was totally devastated.

Legal counsel said it would be an uphill battle because there were few, if any, father's rights in the State of Alabama (at the time). I knew of other fathers that had gone through the system and were still relegated to every other weekends and an occasional weeknight. I didn't know what to do—I missed my daughters desperately, but my whole career had been established and entrenched in Huntsville for the past twelve years. I was in a state of shock, and felt as if my heart had been ripped out. Even if I moved to New Castle, Pennsylvania, I was told that my visitation rights would be limited to the every-other weekend "stuff" and a night during the week. How was I going to start all over again and make a living in a new city, where I didn't know a soul?

I was determined to maintain a relationship with my daughters, and made the trek from Huntsville to New Castle—a small city 60 miles northwest of Pittsburgh—pretty much every other weekend, spending all day to get there and all day to get back. Traveling initially from Huntsville, Alabama, I would sometimes first have to fly to Chicago, Atlanta, Charlotte, Cincinnati or Cleveland, because there weren't any direct flights to Pittsburgh.

I knew all the routes of all the airlines and was determined to keep contact with my daughters. I learned all about frequent flyer miles. Leaving Pittsburgh late Sunday nights, I'd still be wearing my sunglasses to mask the tears that would run easily after saying goodnight to my daughters. I knew it would be another two weeks before I would see them.

I thought this was the worst of times, but this was just the beginning of a very bad patch. Over the next couple of months, my running times worsened, and I was constantly fatigued. I chalked it up to all the activities going on in my life. When I continued to feel weaker and weaker, I decided to quietly get some blood tests. They still showed a relatively low white blood cell count. Having enough white blood cells, and ones that are effective, is important to fight infection. I monitored this over several months and finally called my oncologist friend, Dr. Rich Gualtieri. He suggested a bone marrow biopsy to see what might be going on, which I had on November 5th, 1999.

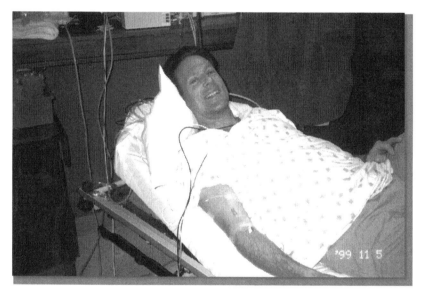

13 days before my diagnosis—November 5th, 1999

The Phone Call

Recalling Chapter 1—on November 18th, 1999, I had just finished the lecture on the "evils" of smoking to some middle school kids. As I drove home, my car phone rang. I answered the call—it was Dr. Rich Gualtieri. "Hi Rich, how are you?" He responded by telling me that there were some "concerning" findings on the bone marrow, and wanted me to come in the next day to discuss it. Immediately, the tone in his voice, the lack of humor, and the word "concerning" instinctively told me it was not good news.

Rich said I had something called MDS—Myelodysplastic Syndrome. I had certainly heard of the disease, but wasn't well versed in it. At that time, MDS wasn't necessarily classified as a form of blood cancer (now it is). Nevertheless, it could eventually destroy all your blood cells—red, white and platelets, and YOU in the process. Rich wanted to see me the next morning in his office.

I didn't get much sleep the night after Rich called me with the results. The rest of that evening was filled with pensive thought and many "what-ifs." The words myelodysplastic syndrome, MDS—resonated in my brain. Not being a hematologist, I didn't know that much about it, only that it could be "very bad."

The next day in Rich's office, he explained my particular situation in detail to me. He was especially concerned about all my infections as well something called Trisomy 8 in my bone marrow—an abnormality in the DNA of bone marrow that is often associated with a malignancy, often a blood cancer. This defect was probably causing my bone marrow to release blood cells before they were fully matured and able to do their job. The immature cells are referred to as "blasts." The number of "blasts" one has—coupled with many other factors—can determine how long one might live. Also, my bone marrow showed "no stainable iron," meaning that iron which is needed to make your red blood cells and other functions work correctly was severely missing—this could be part of the reason I didn't have the energy to run anymore.

MDS are a group of cancers in which bone marrow does not make enough mature, healthy blood cells. They are actually the most common blood cancers in adults, affecting nearly 50,000 Americans every year. MDS patients often need regular blood transfusions, if there red blood cells are affected, for example, to help them fight fatigue and anemia. Some patients are extremely susceptible to infections and their white blood cells are affected (as in my case). They can need antibiotics and other medicines to try to fight off chronic and potentially life threatening infections.

The bottom line with MDS is that the abnormal blood-forming cells in the marrow of the bone aren't working right. Imagine the confusion that patients felt—you have a "terminal" illness but we're not sure how to "label it...or you." Even as a physician, it was very difficult to explain what I had. Today, with the official label of "cancer," in some ways, it's easier to explain. It felt like another weird "label"—like when I was a kid being called "slow"—except this label was lethal.

Seeking Second Opinions

After getting the diagnosis from Rich (who encouraged me to get other opinions as well), I started to educate myself about MDS—who gets it, what is it, how long people might survive. Like many things in my life, I decided to approach it as an obstacle to overcome.

I sought out the best experts in the country, making trips to Vanderbilt Medical Center Department of Hematology and Oncology, City of Hope outside Los Angeles, and consulting with the Mayo Clinic and University of Rochester, NY, with a Dr. John Bennett, a world-renowned expert on MDS and a wonderful doctor. One of the perks of being a surgeon, and having lectured around the country, is that I was extremely fortunate to have access to numerous medical experts.

Dr. Bennett's diagnosis: MDS with "RAEB" classification— meaning refractory anemia with excess blasts—which meant I was potentially a step away from converting to acute leukemia. "You need to stop practicing medicine—it's a hazard to your health," he said, "because exposure to the bacteria you deal with could kill you." I thought back to my life-threatening bout of pneumonia. Again I felt like my head and heart had been smashed.

For one of my consultations, I had flown out to the City of Hope near Los Angeles, a great hospital system that is known for their work on bone marrow transplants. I met with a terrific doctor, Margaret O'Donnell—a hematologist and oncologist. I remember her being warm and compassionate—she spent more than an hour with me on the first visit.

Dr. O'Donnell told me my only chance for a "cure" was a bone marrow transplant. She went through numerous statistics and said that I should immediately be put on the national registry to find a compatible match, if it were even possible. Quickly, I learned that my chances of surviving, according to many, even with a bone marrow transplant, were about 18%. I thought, "You can get better odds in Las Vegas."

In many cases, for a transplant with a person of my age, nearly half of the people never leave the hospital, and another 25% are dead at the end of the first year, with the remaining dying soon after—and that's IF you can find a compatible match.

I left the consultation office and walked down to their spectacular courtyard. I admired the beautiful grounds and sat watching one of the hummingbirds buzz around a feeder—a surreal experience. I was in complete disbelief as I saw several patients rolling their IV polls along as they walked the grounds, and many of them looked like they were more dead than alive.

One of the patients, who had a bone marrow transplant many months before and had survived, struck up a conversation with me. Not knowing what I was facing, he shared with me some of his experiences and said his whole body *"felt like it was on fire"* when he went through something called a bone marrow transplant. He told me he never would have done it had he known the sheer amount of pain he would be going through. It gave me pause for thought—the notion of ever having a total bone marrow transplant was certainly something I wasn't going to consider lightly, if at all.

I continued my journey—getting second, third, and even fourth opinions. None of them were particularly encouraging. Jokingly, I once said to an oncologist, "Can I pick from another category of diseases?" This category wasn't good.

In January 2000, I drove 90 miles north to Nashville to get yet another opinion—from Dr. John Greer, the MDS expert at Vanderbilt University. Dr. Greer also told me to consider a bone marrow transplant. He asked, "Do you have any siblings?" "Yes, one brother," I responded. He said, "Great, we'll send him a special kit to see if he's a match for you." The next visit at Vanderbilt—I was anxiously awaiting to see if my brother Art was a possible donor match—however, the test results were apparently "lost in the mail"—and they promised they'd resend him another test.

A couple of additional weeks went by before I returned to Vanderbilt to finally get the results. I'll never forget sitting in the waiting room. I had a clinical professor of surgery teaching appointment at Vanderbilt, and this waiting room was right next to where I worked with surgical residents. Now I was the patient in the oncology office. The waiting room was full of patients with their loved ones, young and old men and women, most bald from chemotherapy, some with IVs sticking out of them. A man across from me was bald and feverish—he looked half dead. His wife had her arm around him and was rubbing his shoulder reassuringly. I was the only one alone. All I could think was—"I don't want to do any of this." Feeling alone, it reminded me of being that "sick kid" going to the doctors all the time.

Once I was called into see the oncologist again, the look on his face told me all I needed to know. "Your brother isn't even close to being a suitable match," he said. "Also, you really also need to stop practicing surgery and medicine—NOW." A follow up letter from Dr. Greer echoed the other oncologists I had visited—with a cautionary note at the end of having **about two years to live.**

I left Nashville that day feeling worse than I had felt in a long time. On the drive back to Huntsville I put a Harry Chapin song on the cassette player. It was one I played for my kids when I picked them up at the airport called *All My Life's a Circle— Sunrise and Sundown.* The song was all about the stages of life, and I realized that this could be my sundown. Within a year, I would be reading those same lyrics at my mother's funeral and placing them in her coffin. *"Our love is like a circle—Everything has a beginning and an end."*

Vanderbilt Medical Center

Department of Medicine

February 8, 2000

To Whom It May Concern:

Dr. Paul Nemiroff has a diagnosis of myelodysplasia with a cytogenic abnormality (trisomy 8). He has had multiple illnesses including bacterial sepsis... He has functional neutropenia with a decreased myeloid erythroid ratio in his bone marrow.

He is unlikely to mount an adequate white cell response to infections and we are recommending that he discontinue significant direct patient care due to the exposure for infections.

With a cytogenetic abnormality and on pathologist's interpretation as refractory anemia with excess blasts **his median survival is in the two-year range.**

If there are further issues or questions please let us know.

Sincerely,

John P. Greer, M. D.
Division of Hematology Oncology

11

HANGING UP THE SCALPEL

After my diagnosis, I continued working for months, keeping my condition to myself. I seemed to be getting weaker and weaker. I went to my office, drenched in sweat, collapsed on the floor, and felt as if I were burning up. I had a whole room of patients, and I thought, "How can I continue?"

As I had forced myself through so many painful times before, like running marathons, I got up off the floor, rinsed off my face with some cold water, drank a cup of coffee, threw my white coat back on, and finished seeing my clinic of patients. I knew I wasn't contagious to anybody—it was quite the opposite.

I made it through the day, but every step was painful. Every muscle ached and even my skin hurt. It felt as if I had the worst kind of 24/7 flu. The realization came to me that I would need to "hang up my scalpel" very soon—the physical demands were becoming too great.

I finally began to believe that the warning that a number of oncologists had given me—that I needed to quit practicing—was true. Every letter I had received from oncologists said that I was risking my life by continuing to be a surgeon. Simple and pure—the practice of this type of medicine was going to be a hazard to MY health— albeit not to any of my patients.

Interestingly, one of the last patients I treated was a man in his 60s who was in the ER, bleeding out of his eyes, nose, and throat. I packed him to stop the bleeding—everywhere I touched him, his lips, his mucosa in his mouth, he would start bleeding. He was beyond feeling miserable. He told me he had suffered enough and just wanted to go home.

I didn't know his "official" diagnosis, but his tests came back with low platelets, low white counts—I thought he must have leukemia. I called his oncologist.

"It's not leukemia," the oncologist said. "He's got something called MDS. A lot of people haven't heard of it. That's the new term." I checked the man's records. He had been diagnosed a year earlier and he'd been in the hospital many, many times. Suddenly I felt as if I were looking in the mirror—I thought: "I'd take a gun to my head before I'd die like that." After this man was "stabilized," he eventually left the hospital to find peace at home with his wife, family, and other loved ones.

One night in March of 2000, Dr. Jim Garlington, my friend and partner who had already retired from the practice, came to visit me. We had dinner with some other docs that night, and I had to excuse myself because I was white as a ghost and dripping with sweat at the table. Sometime later, Jim said, "Paul, you and I have both seen that *look of death*. You had it that night at the table."

The full gravity of the situation was finally sinking in, but I was numb and still in disbelief that I might soon die. Finally, in about May 2000, and about six months after my original diagnosis, with great sadness, I decided to "retire" from being a surgeon. I left the practice that I had founded and worked so hard to build. I also retired as medical director. It was like going from 100 miles per hour to slamming on the brakes. Suddenly I had nothing to do—but think. And that ticking time bomb inside of me could go off at any time.

Why Not Me?

For the moment I stayed in Huntsville, while I pondered—"Now what?" After getting my diagnosis and being told that I probably only had two years to live, I went through many feelings and thought processes, I guess like all people who are diagnosed with a terminal illness. Various feelings and "stages" of loss and grief—as discussed by the psychologist Dr. Kubler-Ross—are something I experienced: denial—anger, bargaining with God, and sadness went through my mind—but I wasn't ready to "accept" my situation as final, not yet at least. And I don't think I ever asked the question that many others ask—"Why me?"—so much as I asked, "Why not me?"—other than a curiosity about causes of my particular disease.

Was it from fire retardant that I was exposed to as a forest fire fighter in Alaska? Could it have been from radiation that I received while using fluoroscopy as a surgeon? Or had I literally run myself into the ground and damaged my immune system with all the marathons (coupled with my crazy surgical hours). Who knows? I had this label of MDS, and had to deal with it.

To be closer to my daughters, I thought about selling everything and moving to New Castle, Pennsylvania. While living in Huntsville, I was seeing the girls regularly (virtually every other weekend), with flights up to Pittsburgh, then the long drive to New Castle. The town offered me no opportunities to do anything—it was dreary and not somewhere I wanted to be—and I didn't know anybody in New Castle other than my kids.

As I thought about it, I felt it would be a death sentence for me to move there. I was still told I would only be able to see the girls every other weekend (which I was already doing), and once during the week. I feared I would simply die in the small apartment I had rented, with only marginal time with my children, and realized they didn't need me around 24/7—as any parent who reads this knows, kids want you when they want you.

After so many years as a surgeon, I contemplated what my next move might be. As I look back at things today, one of the hardest parts of all the diagnosis and needing to stop operating, perhaps for selfish reasons, was the loss of identity. I'd invested so much of my blood, sweat, tears, and determination to become a surgeon. When I was told that I would increase my chances of dying by being exposed to sick people, and couldn't practice any longer, it was devastating.

As a surgeon you walk a very difficult line. If you shut off your feelings entirely and become just a technician, you might become an arrogant SOB. If you open up your heart and try to feel the pain of others, understanding the families' fears and worries and concerns, and you take this home every night, it could eventually destroy you. The trick is to find the balance. It took me a long time, perhaps 20 years until I thought I found balance—and just as I was finding this balance, I had to hang up my scalpel.

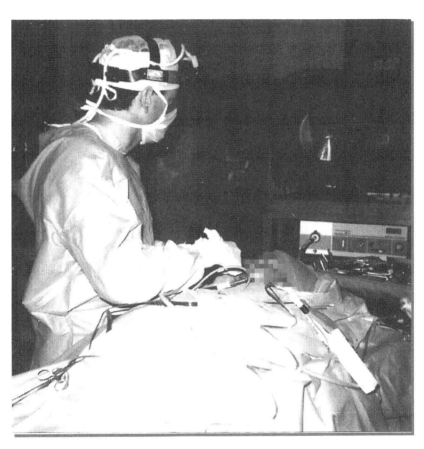

actually this IS brain surgery

12

SEARCHING FOR SOLUTIONS

I began reading, studying, and researching everything I could get my hands on about MDS. I looked at all the theoretical mechanisms of action, of how these "malignant neoplastic clones," as they're called, could form in your bone marrow. I was basically told that the only chance for a cure, as mentioned, was a bone marrow transplant, and that in my particular case, that was a very remote chance.

An interview by the actor Michael Landon (a star in *Bonanza, Little House on the Prairie, Highway to Heaven* and others) came to mind. He knew he was dying from cancer, and rather than being bombarded by the paparazzi every-day, he decided to hold one last "formal" interview at his house. He said something to the effect: "I've had a pretty good run—done a lot of things—can't complain—and know the end is near." Wow, a class act, I thought. I felt like him, to a degree, but wasn't ready to give up just yet. There must be another way. How could I save, or extend my life?

During my surgical training years, I learned about the time in your training when you experience what some surgeons call the

"White Wall Syndrome"—where you turn around to find that the chief resident or attending surgeon (your safety net) has left the operating room. Suddenly you're entirely on your own, with no one to ask, "What do I do now?" if a situation arises. I was now facing the biggest "White Wall" of my medical life. This time, however, I was the patient. It seemed as if all of traditional medicine had "left the room," with few good choices for my terrible diagnosis of MDS. "What do I do now?"

Seating in my "idea chair"—a big tan beauty of a recliner where I'd hatched some great ideas, I came up with some thoughts and "aha" ideas that might make a difference. I'd read a lot about "anti-aging" medicine, about how certain drugs and supplements, can help improve the immune system, at least theoretically.

There are many doctors who are skeptical of many claims made by "anti-aging" physicians. However, knowing that medicine is slow to change, having experienced it myself with some of my ideas, I thought, "Why not give it a chance? What might I learn by going to some of the medical meetings on anti-aging, that also deal with improving one's immune system?" For the orthodox medical community at the time, this was tantamount to heresy—alternative medicine, or complementary medicine, weren't held in high regard by more "traditional" docs.

I knew a fair amount about nutrition and supplements already, not because of any medical training, rather because of my running and studying nutrition on my own, to try to improve performance in marathons. Also, I had recommended many nutritional supplements for my cancer patients over the years, so I had a fairly open mind.

Another very close friend of mine, a surgeon and also a PhD, Dexter Blome, suggested I go to an anti-aging meeting in Las Vegas. Some of the topics at the meeting seemed like total "quackery" to both of us—lotions, potions, and supplements designed to cure "whatever ails you"—a little bit like "snake-oil salesmen" of days gone by.

On the other hand, there were some areas being discussed that had the potential to be "cutting edge." One of these was HGH (Human Growth Hormone) that was being presented by a very reputable physician who said it might boost the immune system. That got my attention.

As I spoke with some of the "real scientists" there, and further to Dexter, I thought this HGH stuff may be of benefit to me, and others—not as a "performance enhancing" drug or to try to "keep me young," but rather as something that, based on many research articles, suggested it could help one's immune system when taken in the proper doses—and perhaps might even extend cell life, and be the "spark" that potentially could extend my life. I recognized all of this was still conjecture to a degree, but the science and theories behind this were intriguing.

I needed a prescribing physician. HGH was only approved for use in children with growth disorders, and for people with growth hormone deficiencies—anything else was an "off-label" prescription. Again, I was not looking to use it as a "performance-enhancing" drug, nor as a way to try and stay "young"—as is touted in many pop culture articles—but simply to put my HGH levels back to perhaps when I was 35 or so, in a way that might boost my immune system.

Scientists do know that enhancing one's immune system is a

central theme in fighting diseases of virtually any kind. I spoke with Dexter, who was familiar with HGH and knew of a number of anecdotal stories of where it helped patients who had both chronic diseases—e.g. liver problems, and other maladies.

"We're friends," he said, but he was nervous about prescribing it to me—would it make my cancer possibly grow faster? I explained I was willing to take the chance at that point. He agreed, and after signing a release saying that I knew the treatment might theoretically make my disease worse, and after a number of blood tests, he wrote the prescription and I added daily HGH injections to my antioxidant, anti-inflammatory, and potentially "anti-cancer" supplement regimen that I developed.

I then made an appointment to be examined by some physicians who had a lot of knowledge about HGH and other supplements for "anti-aging" or "age management," as they liked to call it—a place called Cenegenics® in Las Vegas, Nevada. Cenegenics did an entire blood analysis and physical exam, then suggested some additional changes to the protocol I was already on. They too, and appropriately so, were nervous about giving this "stuff" to someone with an active malignancy.

Again, after signing release papers, I began using a number of additional supplements, as well as HGH and other substances. I continued my studies on supplements and their potential anti-cancer, anti-inflammatory, and anti-oxidant properties. New research has shown that inflammation in the body can promote arthritis, heart disease, and even cancer. Many scientists believe that inflammation is the "root of all evil." Preventing or reducing inflammation, in certain situations, may be life-saving and "life-extending."

Of course, none of this had been absolutely proven in a double-blind, randomized, gold-standard trials yet, with respect to extending life—but I didn't have time to wait. I believed that it might actually help, because the research I was reviewing suggested that many of these substances may not only have anti-cancer effects, but at least in "petri-dish" experiments, they may extend the life of cells.

When I shared this with some of my oncologist friends, they were horrified and said, "This could really give you cancer and spread it, and actually shorten your life span." My response: "Have you read any of the latest experimental research with supplements and growth hormone?" Most hadn't. They were "experts" in their own field, and frankly there are only so many hours in the day, and many docs don't have time to always read the latest journals, or especially those that are "outside" traditional medicine. To his credit, Dr. Rich Gualtieri, who first diagnosed me, kept an open mind, especially since he believed a bone marrow transplant was too risky.

I was already told I had maybe only two years to live anyway. I don't want to sound cavalier here, but I didn't want to just wait around, and I DID want to look at some alternative treatments, as do, I suppose, many patients who are diagnosed with a terminal disease.

With many of the anti-aging programs and meetings being held in Las Vegas at the time, maybe I would have better odds in Vegas after all? Especially with the extraordinary risks (and low odds of survival) of a bone marrow transplant for my situation— oh yes, and there weren't even any donors available that came close to matching my "unique" genetic code at that time. It's nice to be unique, I guess—but sometimes you want to say: *"Really?!"*

Two Things to Know

After I came to the realization that I had to "hang up my scalpel," I was faced with an even more daunting task—trying to save my own life. Having been involved in one form of research or another for most of my career, I decided to investigate many of the theories of what causes cancer, traditional treatments, and alternative therapies, including some notions, which were extremely provocative.

Over time, I developed a theory and protocol—an amalgamation of the work of many others. I believe it has kept me alive all these years and against all odds. Some of these ideas are very controversial, and many were followed, in some cases, against the recommendations of my oncologists. In no way do these theories or treatments discount traditional treatments for cancer, such as surgery, radiation, or chemotherapy. But facing a ticking time bomb, with no cure, what did I have to lose? And there were hundreds of studies suggesting the potential benefits of these supplements. [see Appendix for more specifics]

My attorneys have advised me that I must include another disclaimer at this point, to say, **"Always check with your own physician or healthcare professional before taking any supplements or medications."** I must emphasize: I was carefully monitored by several physicians, and of course a number of the treatments in the protocol I use, do require a prescription.

On a very simplistic level, there are at least two things you need to know about any cancer (recognizing that cancer is not just one disease):

(1) How to stop it from starting;

(2) If it's already started, how to slow it down.

It has long been known that our immune system, a complex network of checks and balances in the body, protects us and helps prevent us from catching any disease, including cancer—that is, when it's fully functional, fully intact, and running, if you will, on all 8 cylinders.

However, there are many forces that can break down our immune system and cause it to malfunction. These can include everything from infections, to environmental toxins, to hereditary conditions. Trauma, stress, excessive inflammation in the body, poor diet, or poor lifestyle choices can also do it. With that said, the two prongs of the "model" (albeit very simplistic) are:

Prong 1: Boost the immune system to reduce the chances of ever catching a disease, or cancer. Also, by boosting the immune system, your body may be able to heal itself, so it can help the killer T cells fight infections, and help other cells fight against cancer cells. To my physician colleagues out there, I know that this is a highly simplified explanation, and that there are a plethora of "mechanisms of action," as we docs like to say. This, of course, is more of a "big picture" view that I'm trying to convey to non-medical folks.

Prong 2: "Free radicals" are damaging substances that can cause "apoptosis"—or cell death. With too many free radicals, all sorts of maladies can occur, from heart disease, to arthritis, to cancer. There's a theoretic basis that these "bullies of the body"—a term I coined—can be counter-acted with anti-oxidants—powerful substances that fight against the damage done by free radicals. In a way, they may help prevent the oxidation, or "rust," that occurs inside (and on the outside) of your body. These anti-oxidants in essence, try to neutralize free radicals (and in a way, "quench" some of the inflammation), so that they don't do harm to your body. This can help protect your DNA—the "blueprint" for making new cells. DNA mutations—for example, in the simplest of terms, can be described in the following analogy. Instead of your bone marrow "typing in" a genetic code of ABC, it types in ABD, or ABE. The copies just aren't right, and cell function can be altered, which could potentially lead to cancer.

I've put these two principles to use, given my situation with MDS, because I had little to lose, and much to potentially gain. There's always a risk-benefit ratio, and I felt the risks, in my case, were low for any damage, and the potential benefits huge. **Again, I'm not recommending that anyone start this protocol without checking with their own physician and getting the proper monitoring, as I have.**

I didn't discard more traditional therapies either. When I had a bacterial infection, I was immediately placed on antibiotics, because my white cells weren't functioning properly. Also I used a "chemo agent" to stimulate white cells—Neupogen® (generic name: filgrastim) produced by Amgen. I'm convinced that, many times, my Neupogen shots helped me get over or prevent a life-threatening infection.

Through my research, I developed a daily protocol. There are a host of anti-oxidants, supplements, and medications I use. It's amazing to what length one might go to save one's life. My protocol is described in detail in this book's Appendix.

13

BREAKING NEWS

When I realized that being a surgeon and exposing myself to infectious diseases was now critically perilous to my health, I sought another way to try and stay involved with medicine, without the risks to my well being.

It was a warm summer in 2000. While sitting in my "famous recliner chair," which had birthed many ideas and inventions in the past, I came up with another idea whereby I could still keep my hands in medicine in some way, not only by lecturing and consulting, but by being a TV Medical Correspondent.

I was watching some young local health reporter talking about an issue in medicine, and she wasn't doing a very good job. She was mispronouncing words, like *ma-sect-omy* instead of mastectomy, and *prostrate* vs. prostate. I realized she wasn't a doctor or nurse and didn't know what she was talking about. I thought, "I can do this, and I could do it better. How tough could it be?" After all, as I would come to learn a saying in TV, "It's not brain surgery or rocket science"—and I actually had some experience in both those fields.

Just like every other career to date, I thought, "What do I have to fear?" (except perhaps taking a standardized test)—

especially given my life circumstance, it might be a "short gig" anyway. What the heck? I had no idea about the TV industry and what was involved, but was determined to learn. I thought the best place to learn about this would be close to where my daughters lived, near Pittsburgh. Naïve about the industry, I thought I could simply call each station around the Pittsburgh area and see if they had any interest in hiring me as a TV medical reporter. Pittsburgh was a pretty large market, #20 in the country at the time out of 210. My phone calls weren't even returned.

Undeterred, I started to call local stations in Huntsville, Alabama. The first station I called actually gave me an interview and the news director told me, "You don't have any experience, but we'll give you a chance. Come over in a few days and we'll talk about it." A few days later, I returned for a follow-up interview. The news director who I'd spoken with had been fired the day before, and a new person was there. The new guy on the block said, "We're not hiring anyone now." Later I learned that news directors, not unlike NFL football players, usually had a very short career lifetime, somewhere in the two-year range, on average.

I continued calling stations in Huntsville and eventually got an interview at WAAY TV—the ABC affiliate (the #81 market in the country). Again, the news director was reluctant to hire me. He was unimpressed by my resume or surgical skill, because this had little to do with being good "on air."

He said, "You haven't got any TV experience, do you?"

I responded, "Well, I watch TV."

His arms remained crossed, not amused by my answer. He was very ho-hum, saying, "We'll get back to you."

Suddenly, I heard my name though the open door: "Hey Dr. Nemiroff," someone said. I turned. It was the general manager of the station—he had been a patient of mine sometime before. He told the news director that I was a "good guy" and said, "Let's give him a shot." WAAY TV was where I would cut my teeth as a medical correspondent—*"Health Beat" on Tuesdays and Thursdays with Dr. Paul Nemiroff.*

I knew nothing about "sound bites" or "packages"—or much of anything about TV, but I started researching it, as I do with all my "new projects." The weekend before I was supposed to be on the air, my daughters were with me for the weekend to celebrate one of their birthdays. Everything was going great, and I was going to take them to the airport a couple days later, then start my TV career on Tuesday. But every time you think you have it all planned, life can throw you a curveball. As someone once said, "If you want to make God smile, just tell him what your plans are."

The day before my first airing, and just after the birthday party, I received a horrible call from California from my brother Art. He said, "You'd better get to LA fast. Mom had a massive stroke and was hospitalized in a coma. She's probably not going to make it."

I needed to get out there immediately. I rushed my daughters to Nashville Airport, where they could get a non-stop flight to Pittsburgh, and stayed with them until they got on board. Minutes later I was able to catch the last flight to Los Angeles. I called the TV station and told them what was going on, and they understood. The promotion they had done, and my first "featured airing" were now insignificant to me.

Arriving late at LAX that night, I headed right to the hospital and met my brother and sister-in-law. They hadn't seen the attending doctor. My Mom was in a coma and fighting for her life. I called her attending physician, who was nowhere to be found. Knowing my way around hospitals, and putting on the surgeon hat, and a white coat, I walked into the X-ray department and asked one of the residents there to see the scans of my Mom, without telling them my relationship to her. One look at her CT scans showed a massive bleed into her brain, and made me realize that her chances of survival were not good.

I was less than thrilled with the care she received at that institution. For the record, the attending female physician who was taking care of my Mom never once spoke with me in person. Even after my Mom passed, the doctor never once called or came to talk with me, or my family—and I was at the hospital nearly 24/7. No wonder doctors get sued. This wasn't the kind of quality of care I always strived to provide—compassion and face-to-face meetings with *every patient*—because they deserve it.

My Mom survived for several more days, although the bleeding continued to wipe out her brain. She never woke up. My brother Art and sister-in-law Ute were there from the beginning and were very stressed. They didn't want to see the tubes, and couldn't see her like that any longer, and finally left for the day. After looking at the deterioration under scans, I made sure the doctors provided her medicine so she wouldn't suffer, and she drifted off into complete unresponsiveness.

I remember the last time with my Mom, holding her hand, and being the only one in the room. I'd never told my Mom about my diagnosis, not wanting her to worry. I remember telling her that night that I would see her again sometime, and it was OK to let go. I went out of the room to get some water, and when I came back, she had passed on. Even in her death, she didn't want to bother her son with dying in front of me. She had led a long life of 80 years. But no matter what age you are, it's tough to lose your Mom.

Years earlier, my colorblind brother Art and I had bought our Mom a mismatched kelly green purse for her birthday, thinking it was brown and would match her brown shoes. On this occasion of our Mom's funeral, we achieved full circle, purchasing a bright burnt orange casket, which we both thought was brown. This caused a few raised eyebrows from visitors, but we knew our Mom would be smiling.

On The Air

Still reeling from the loss of my mother, a week later I made it back to Huntsville and embarked on a new career in TV. My first story was about the effects of cell phones on the brain, and whether it might cause brain cancer.

On the TV set, the director counted off, "3...2...1..." and the anchors started talking—I was in the next TV "block," a few minutes later. My heart was racing. My mouth was dry. I was incredibly nervous. As a surgeon, I'd held a beating heart in my hand, performed brain surgery, and operated on gunshot wounds to the face. I'd truly dealt with life and death situations—but this was different. I was totally out of my element.

As the news anchor did her "toss" to me, the camera swung in my direction, and the only thing that could calm me down was thinking my Mom was watching and thought I was doing a good job. I really didn't know what I was doing, and wasn't particularly good, but had some natural talent, so I was told—especially "on the fly" (as they say in TV land—meaning being able to be spontaneous).

I continued to improve—every Tuesday and Thursday it was *"Health Beat with Dr. Nemiroff." One* of the early stories I did was about a new pair of glasses for colorblind people—to allow them to "see" colors—much like the red lens I wore, at times, as a surgeon. They looked like cool sunglasses.

The whole point of the piece was that kids who are colorblind may be labeled as "stupid" (a term that actually was often used in the past) or "slow" in grammar school, because so many learning tools are color-coded—like when the teacher asks the children to pick up a red circle and the colorblind child picks up a yellow one—or simply isn't sure. Doing this story was like telling the story of my own misunderstood childhood, my colorblindness. "Paul, you need to learn your colors better," as one teacher said, not understanding that I literally couldn't see certain colors.

On my show, I did feature stories about new tests and treatments for prostate cancer, breast cancer, and back pain—all the standard stuff. As I gained more experience, I did more and more on the fly, engaging in dialogue with the news anchors.

A Fresh Start

Since I had a bit of TV experience in Alabama on the local ABC affiliate, I decided to make a five-minute resume tape—*"The Best of Health Beat"*—and sent it to all the stations in Pittsburgh and about a 200-mile radius, including several cities in Ohio: Youngstown, Cleveland, Columbus, and Cincinnati. All of these were within driving distance of my kids in New Castle, Pennsylvania. I thought, "Maybe I could get a TV gig in one of these cities and be nearer to them."

I didn't know anything about market size, or prestige, or anything. I just wanted to do something that gave me some sort of purpose in life, and still have access to my daughters on a regular basis, and be closer to them. However, a station in Pittsburgh made the comment, "You have no real experience—this is a 'big market'—#20 out of 210. Huntsville's #81 and you need a lot of experience to get here."

Eventually, I did get a few interviews in Youngstown and in Columbus, but still no bites in Pittsburgh. After each of the interviews in these cities, it was "Don't call us, we'll call you." Later, I would come to realize that even getting an interview was an accomplishment. But there were no further returned phone calls from any of the stations in Pittsburgh or the 200-mile surrounding area.

It took me about eight hours door-to-door to get from Huntsville, Alabama to New Castle, Pennsylvania. Whether flying through Atlanta, Charlotte, or Chicago—you name it—I knew the ways to get to Pittsburgh. Soon I realized that it took less than eight hours door-to-door to see my kids from LA—because of all the direct flights available. Also, LA was familiar to me because it's where I'd grown up. I felt that, after the best and worst of times over thirteen years in Huntsville, it was the right moment to leave and get "a fresh start."

While I hadn't had any luck getting into the Pittsburgh or

Ohio TV markets, I decided I would try to get a gig in Southern California. It's good that I had NO IDEA about how difficult it is to get on air at the #2 station in the country, Los Angeles. Some people in TV spend their entire careers trying to move up the "food chain," or market size.

I sent my resume (aka "brag sheet") and my 5-minute resume tape to all the stations in the LA area, and to my surprise, all three of the major networks there—CBS, ABC, and NBC— responded. While I couldn't get the time of day with much smaller stations in Ohio and Pittsburgh, the three "big dogs" in LA had interest. I set up some interviews and headed from The Deep South back to my hometown in "the land of milk and honey."

KCBS LA

My first interview in LA was September 10th, 2001 at KCBS. The news director there, Roger Bell, said he would give me 10 minutes, so "come on over." Instead of 10 minutes, an hour and half went by on the first visit. He said he'd looked at my resume tape, and although it was pretty raw, he saw some natural talent. He told me, "I'll get back to you." I expected the usual, "Don't call me, we'll call you," routine.

I returned to my hotel that evening near Los Angeles Airport and had some other TV meetings that were re-scheduled for a week or so later. Therefore, I thought I would head to Pittsburgh the next morning to see my kids. Of course, we all know how the world changed forever on the next day, September 11th, 2001. Obviously all other upcoming meetings were cancelled with the TV stations—they had bigger things to deal with. The early flight

I'd planned at LAX was cancelled, and every other airport was shut down. I returned to the hotel and was spellbound as TV stations relived the horror of the twin towers coming down. My first thought was how to get back to see my kids.

Realizing the airport would be shut down indefinitely, I thought maybe there was some way I could help in New York. I called the Director of Surgery at Cedars-Sinai to see if they might be sending a team of surgeons to Ground Zero to help, and offered to volunteer—knowing that I would put myself at some risk, but I felt I had to do something.

They were in fact looking for volunteers, and explained that since all the airports had been shut down, they were trying to arrange a military flight of surgeons—possibly from Edward's Air Force Base (recalling *Venture One*—the granddaddy rocket I had launched there as a kid). They took my cell number and said they'd be in touch as soon as more information became available.

After a day or two stuck at the hotel, watching the same clips on TV over and over again, I received a phone call from Cedars-Sinai about New York. They had no idea how many were dead, and were told by hospital officials in New York that they wouldn't need help—since they weren't finding many survivors. At one point, there was a fear that 50,000 could have been killed. Fortunately this wasn't the case, but the tragedy was nevertheless etched in my brain, as I'm sure it was for most Americans.

When the airport in LA finally reopened, I got the first flight out to Pittsburgh to see my kids. The plane was essentially empty. When I got to Pittsburgh, I went through my ritual of renting a car and driving 45 miles north to New Castle. The apartment was, shall we say, a less-than-fancy single-bedroom "dump," which my kids and I ironically dubbed "The Mansion."

The Mansion was clean and well lit, had a tiny cook's galley, and all the basic necessities. Over the years, I spent many weekends in that little apartment making memories with my two daughters. Each kid had their own little mattress in one corner of the room, while I slept in what was essentially a large closet. We built "volcanoes" for science projects, carved out pumpkins for Halloween, and most importantly, I continued trying to build my relationship with my daughters. At the time, my feeling was that they were too young to be told about their Dad facing a terminal illness. And most of the time I looked "healthy." Quietly though, there were many days when my fatigue was overwhelming—but I hid it from people the best I could.

After going back to Pittsburgh post-9/11, and while driving on the Pennsylvania Turnpike (which is known for areas with spotty cell phone coverage), I received a call from Roger Bell at CBS. He asked, "Paul, are you interested in giving it a shot as a medical correspondent?" Just as I was starting to get excited, in mid-conversation, my phone went dead. Finally, after a couple of frantic hours, we re-connected. I was eventually offered a spot as the Chief Medical Correspondent for CBS television in LA— KCBS. Roger jokingly told me, "We'll put you on at 2 a.m. to start, so if you really screw up, you can disappear quickly. No big deal, we'll just fire you." Fortunately, that never happened.

It was a huge opportunity. I went back to Huntsville, said my goodbyes, and moved to Southern California. I didn't want to live in the middle of LA, which can be a zoo, so I moved to Newport Beach in Orange County, about an hour away from KCBS. My brother and sister-in-law lived near there, as did one of my nieces, Lysa. I rented a condo and commuted the 50 miles each way to the station.

Newport Beach is a spectacular area of the country—beautiful climate, beautiful beaches, "beautiful people." However, I had never seen so many "enhancement" procedures on women in my life. It seemed as if every other girl had something adjusted, implanted, or re-aligned. I remember doing a story about plastic surgery and asking a young woman why she was undergoing so many procedures. She said she was turning 26 the next year, and had to keep up with the 22 year-olds. The standard joke in Newport was: "If there is ever a flood, all the women here will float."

At the time, I only knew one person in Newport, Ron Sechrist—the owner of Sechrist Industries, which makes hyperbaric units. I'd met him many years before at medical conventions, and over the years we became friends. He told me to call him when I got there, and was very kind and generous, introducing me to many people. Ron told me I had to meet one guy in particular, Dr. Michael Spitzer—aka "Dr. Mike"—a well-known dentist in town who seemed to know everybody. Seeing what a good father Dr. Mike was to his daughter is one of the reasons that I liked him so much, and to this day we are close friends. Mike introduced me to the nightlife and social events in Newport—*yikes*.

While in the Newport area, I also met a guy named Steve Gross—a colorful man, generous to a fault, full of life, and also a terrific father. He was the former CEO of Thrifty Rent-a-Car and would always insist on giving me a "complimentary" car when flying back into LAX. He too has remained a life-long friend and has been there for me through the best and worst of times.

I continued my every-other-weekend flight from LAX or John Wayne Airport to Pittsburgh to spend 48 hours with my daughters. I would fly out on a Friday, get in late, pick them up and take them to "The Mansion." Then on Sunday I would kiss them goodnight and head back, either on an overnight or early morning flight, to get me back into LA in time for my TV gig. It was a gut-wrenching ritual every time. It would take a few hours for my daughters to warm up to me, then things were OK—only to leave again and not see them for another couple of weeks.

Media Power

One of my first pieces on the live set in Los Angeles was with two seasoned anchors, Ann Martin and Harold Green, legends in the area. Within my first week or two, there were some "technical difficulties." Half of the time, I didn't know which camera to look at, because there's a red light that comes on to tell you which one is "hot"—and obviously that posed another colorblind challenge.

While doing a piece on breast cancer, I turned to the teleprompter and the wrong graphics came up—it was Los Angeles weather. Fortunately, Harold and Ann bailed me out from my "deer in the headlights" look that I must have displayed. I recovered quickly and began ad-libbing (since I'd researched the piece carefully), and it all worked. After the newscast, everyone said I had handled it well "on the fly." They told me I was a natural on air and that I seemed to connect with the audience. The news director was impressed, and I now had a real gig. I was off and running in the "TV big leagues."

You can never predict how a bend in life's road will lead you to your ultimate calling. Had I not gotten MDS, I might still be operating, or retired. Facing a ticking time clock fundamentally changed the way I looked at the world, and led me on my quest to save my own life (at first), and now perhaps the lives of many others.

I was chatting with Dr. Art Ulene, a former UCLA Bruin and long time former medical correspondent of The Today Show. He was *"The TV Doctor"* for 20 years. When I got started in TV, I called him for some advice. He asked me, "Paul, how many patients have you worked on?"

With a bit of thought, I replied, "About 35,000."

Next he asked, "How many surgeries have you done?"

I said, "About 10,000."

"Think about this," Art said, "even on a night with poor ratings, you'll reach more people on CBS than you may have helped in your entire career."

That thought kept me going—maybe there was power in the media after all. I continued doing various medical stories for KCBS—one on snoring and sleep apnea included a "live chat" after the airing. Four computers were set up to answer questions from viewers after the piece was "on air"—I would respond to the producers, who would then email back the answers in "real time." After about ten minutes, the station received so many calls and emails—in the thousands—that the system shut down. This meant people were watching.

My big coup at KCBS was a story about a new treatment for babies born with a hole in their heart. The treatment eliminated the need for surgically opening the baby's chest. In involved inserting a surgical catheter into a vein in the baby's groin, running it up to the heart, and closing the hole between the chambers. Cedars-Sinai Medical Center was one of the first places doing it—it was easy for me to gain access to hospitals, because I wasn't just a "health reporter"—but a surgeon turned medical correspondent, which opened many doors.

My segment showed a toddler who was bed-ridden and didn't have the breath or energy to walk. The day after the new procedure, the kid was running around in his diapers and playing games. The story won me the Surgeon General's C. Everett Koop Media 1st place award for Best TV Medical Feature, presented by the American Heart Association. Suddenly I was an "Award-winning TV medical correspondent."

Close to the Bone

Reviewing the news feeds and breaking medical announcements each day was exciting. In the media, you frequently get information before it's even published in a journal—and there is an embargo until you are allowed to release it as "breaking news."

On one occasion, a particular story really caught my attention—one that I knew something about—and was "close to the bone" so to speak. It was on a drug—thalidomide—being used to help patients with MDS. This was the same drug that, back in the 1960s, was used with pregnant women to help with morning sickness—until it was discovered that it caused terrible deformities in thousands of newborns, including some who were born with "seal type limbs." Thalidomide was quickly removed from the market in other countries—although as a credit to our FDA, the drug was never approved in the United States.

In recent years, though, thalidomide was now being explored to treat leprosy, multiple myeloma, and MDS. The drug has properties that could inhibit new blood vessels—cutting off blood supply to tumors—and could boost red blood cell production, thus MDS patients with this problem could possibly require fewer transfusions. It was a great story: *"The drug that once caused horrific birth defects was now improving rather than ruining lives."* Of course, I had a special interest.

Interviewing the oncologist at Hoag hospital in Newport Beach, he was very nice to me—I thought he was just "making nice" because the story was going to be good publicity for the hospital. It turned out he had been a medical student at UCLA when I was there. "You were so kind to me," he said, "showing me stuff—and explaining things. I've never forgotten that."

The camera crew came down and we did the story. After interviewing the patients and hearing about some of the drug's benefits, and its side effects—ranging from shortness of breath to severe constipation and fatigue—I hoped I wouldn't need that drug. At the time, my problem was primarily with my white blood cells, not the red blood cells that thalidomide might help.

Of course, I interviewed the heck out of this oncologist. He said, "For a head and neck surgeon, you sure know a lot about MDS." He had no idea, nor did anyone at the TV station or in California (except my brother and sister-in-law), about my medical condition.

It happened to be about time for another checkup of myself—and I asked him if I could speak with him privately. After the camera crews left, I asked him to guarantee the "Doctor-Patient relationship"—then told him I had MDS. He was stunned and his face dropped.

"But you look healthy," he said. "How long has it been since you were diagnosed and what stage?"

I told him the details and eventually became his patient for a time. Because I was having more night sweats, fevers, and other symptoms, and some blood work that wasn't quite right, he recommended another bone marrow biopsy.

"Okay," I said.

When the results came back, I was shocked. He told me that it looked like one out of every four or five of my red blood cells had two nuclei—almost like having "two heads" to them instead of one—meaning they were starting to look weird—or "funky" (not a medical term). The red blood cells hadn't been affected before, but they were now.

There was more bad news on my Trisomy 8 abnormality as well. Instead of two malignant clones in the bone marrow, there were now five—the percent of DNA damage had gone up—not a particularly good finding. I then told him about my treatment regimen with HGH injections, testosterone, and antioxidants. Like several of my oncologists, he said, "Your protocol might be speeding up your disease."

"Yeah," I said, "but it's been about two years. Maybe that's just the natural progression?"

Or maybe it wasn't. I continued with my protocol, always researching and studying about anti-oxidants, supplements, and growth hormones. While I had real concerns—there wasn't much else I could do that was shown to really extend life for MDS patients at the time—except a bone marrow transplant—and that was off the list. The few drugs available to help with some symptoms weren't without major risks, and weren't suited for my case.

It was time to make some more decisions and to head closer to my kids. I put another resume tape together (from CBS in LA where I was working) and sent it to all the stations in Pittsburgh, hoping to get a gig in that city—and this time it worked. I'd gone from being an "unknown in TV" to someone who was being courted by the top three stations in Pittsburgh. After being at the big station in LA, they thought: "Hey, he must be good." I found it quite ironic—just a year earlier, I couldn't get the time of day from anyone in the Pittsburgh or surrounding area.

After interviews with various TV stations in Pittsburgh, I liked KDKA, the CBS affiliate, the most, and decided to accept a position there. I gave my notice in LA and told them I was moving "Back East." People wondered why I would "step down" from such a big deal as CBS in LA to a much smaller market in Pittsburgh at KDKA. No one knew about my illness—but it was never about market size or prestige. I wanted something to keep my mind occupied, to keep my hand in medicine (bringing useful medical reports to people), and most importantly to be in closer proximity to my kids—the every-other-weekend cross-country flights were killing me.

Most of all, the feeling of a "hole in my heart," without some normal existence with my daughters, became overwhelming. That, coupled with the fact that I felt like I was living on a time-bomb that could go off any minute with respect to my MDS, compelled me to get closer to my kids, and still have some form of life for myself.

14

THE BURGH

A buddy of mine from my PhD days, Dr. Tom Ollerman, ("But that's OK"—*see Chapter 3 @ Purdue*) drove from Phoenix to Newport to help me pack up the rest of my things and ship them to New Castle, Pennsylvania. After saying my goodbyes to a few friends in Newport, I traversed the country with plenty of time to think as I made my way across nine states in my old 1995 BMW, with a week's worth of HGH (human growth hormone) safe in a cold pack beside me, along with all my other "protocol" nutritional supplements and medicines.

I'd moved so many times before—this seemed like a really good one, because I would be so close to my daughters, and I had a job waiting. Entering the summer of 2002, I knew where I was going, and yet I had no idea what lay ahead. Not really. Looking back, I never could have guessed what was to come. Never in a million years.

When I arrived in New Castle, Pennsylvania, I stayed at "The Mansion," my humble apartment. Meanwhile, I sought to find a new place to live close enough to my kids, and also close enough to the TV station, about 60 miles away. I decided on a small community in Western Pennsylvania about halfway between KDKA and New Castle on an Arnold Palmer designed golf course (although I don't play golf). The location was called Treesdale—some years before, it was simply a beautiful apple orchard with winding pathways through rolling hills.

I remember the first time I visited on a spectacular September day, 68 degrees. Fog was rolling in such a way you could almost imagine an ocean in the distance. For a moment, it reminded me of Newport Beach—fresh, clean, beautiful. Little did I know that this beautiful fall day would be short-lived—a freezing cold winter was coming.

Having interviewed at KDKA a few months before, I was unaware that a couple of the male anchors thought I might be a potential replacement for them. The news director there, a guy named Al Blinke, seemed to get some enjoyment out of not telling the male anchors what my real role was going to be. He told me: "It helps to keep them on their toes." Finally, Al told everybody they had hired a new Medical Correspondent. I started working at KDKA three to four days a week, which allowed me more time to spend with my kids. Frankly, I also didn't have the energy to work every day. Symptoms of fatigue, night sweats, and other things persisted.

Interestingly I was supposed to start on September 3rd, but because I was still in transition, I asked if I could start a few weeks later, on September 23rd, 2002. Years later, I would realize this was the exact month and day that my future wife had started at KDKA, many years earlier—no coincidences.

On my first day at KDKA, everyone came up and introduced themselves to me. They were friendly, considerate, kind, and I thought, "What a wonderful place to work." Many referred to me as "Dr. Paul"—a nickname which started many years before. Maybe this was because my last name Nemiroff was difficult to spell and pronounce for some people. In fact, it wasn't uncommon for me to be paged over the loud speaker at the hospital as "Dr. Demerol." Other fascinating pronunciations were: Dr. Ni-mier-ov — Dr. Nem-ross — Dr. Nem-rod — Dr. Nem — or even "Nem." Of course, I was often confused with the vodka Smirnoff®. Today there's a very famous Ukrainian vodka called Nemiroff®—same spelling (hopefully some distant relative will send me a few free samples).

The main anchor at KDKA, a legend at the station and rated as one of the top anchors of all the CBS affiliates, was a woman named Patrice King Brown. Everybody seemed to love Patrice, both in and outside of the station. She made a point of introducing herself to me and was very polite and cordial.

Giving Thanks

My first Thanksgiving night in Pittsburgh in 2002, I had nowhere to go. I'd just quietly celebrated on November 18th, my third year since being diagnosed with MDS and estimated only two years to live—so I was thankful to still be here having at least an extra year, but I felt incredibly lonely. My kids were having dinner with their mom.

One person at the station (the Consumer Reporter) always very nice—her name was Yvonne, and she happened to be close friends with Patrice. Patrice was having Thanksgiving with her kids, so Yvonne invited me to her house to celebrate the holiday with her husband and family. Yvonne prepared an elaborate feast and it was a great party. Who could have known that Yvonne's days were numbered as well—several years later she succumbed to ovarian cancer—but that night she and her family made me feel welcome in such a special way—thank you Yvonne.

As I left Yvonne's house around 8:30 p.m. I realized that I wasn't far from where Patrice lived, so I called and asked if she'd like to get together for a drink after the Thanksgiving festivities. We met at Southwest Mall, after I followed her 'Pittsburgeese' directions—i.e. "Turn left at the old Isaly's"—street names are seldom referenced, as opposed to locally known landmarks. Then she took me to one her favorite spots in her hometown—Mt.

Washington with its commanding view of downtown and the convergence of three major rivers. Patrice looked out across the skyline with pride and announced, "This is my city."

Woman Of The Year

Patrice and I started dating after Thanksgiving. Just before New Years I saw her number pop up on my cell phone and I answered. "Guess who you're talking to?" "Umm," I replied, not sure if this was some kind of trick question. "This year's *Woman of the Year*—it's a black tie event and you have to be there."

In January 2003 Patrice was honored by the City of Pittsburgh, winning the *"Woman of the Year Award."* They were honoring people in a variety of categories—business, religion, architects—who epitomized the skills or abilities in their profession, gave back to the community, donated their time, and served on non-profit boards. Her award was for the field of Communications, as she celebrated her 25th year at KDKA with ratings among the highest in the country.

I was in a new tux for the event, although Patrice's son Guy was "officially" her escort to the event. Guy sat at the front table with all the honorees and I sat at another table with Patrice's daughter Lauren, her boyfriend Steve, and the KDKA people. After the gala event, we all went downstairs into the swanky hotel and again toasted to Patrice. It was an honor to be the date of the night's honoree.

Telling Patrice

Over time Patrice became a close friend and confidante, and our platonic relationship was blossoming into a romantic one. As we came to understand and know each other, one night I shared with her my "secret" about my having a terminal illness. It was a tremendous relief to be able to share this with someone I completely trusted, and someone with whom I was falling in love. I never felt judged by Patrice, nor did I feel I would be abandoned.

Every so often, during a break between telecasts at KDKA, Patrice and I would go out for dinner. On one of our "dates," I asked her, "What would you do if you were told you had two years to live?" Patrice thought for a moment, then replied, "I would probably travel and see the world, and spend time with my children." We spoke for a bit about where she would travel, and at the time she didn't ask me the same question in return.

One evening, after a particularly bad day that left me feeling distraught, I invited Patrice to dinner at a local restaurant called Atrias. She had only an hour for the meal before having to get back to KDKA to do a "cut in," so we got in her car and headed out. As we drove across the bridge past the PNC Park (home of the Pittsburgh Pirates), she could tell that I was fidgeting in discomfort.

As Patrice parked the car I asked her, "Could we talk for a minute?" She nodded, and I continued "I want to share something with you. And I really need your trust." Patrice said, "What you don't know about me, because you don't know me well, is that you can trust me. This will not go anywhere."

I took a deep breath and went on. "Remember a few months

ago when I asked you about the question about what you would do if you found out you had two years to live?" I saw the expression in her face turn to fear and could feel my heart racing, my mouth getting dry.

Not wanting to be interrupted, I continued, "I don't know if I can go through all this, but here goes. One of the reasons I didn't want to allow myself to get too close to you is because—I didn't think I would be around too long. About two years ago I was diagnosed with a form of blood cancer and the prognosis isn't particularly good. The doctors said I'd only have about two years to live. I'm reportedly pushing the limit already"

Patrice was visibly stunned, and reached over and grabbed my hand, a tear rolling down her right cheek. I swallowed hard and told her I had undergone recent tests, and although things were fairly stable, some findings said my disease was going in the wrong direction. I knew Patrice cared about me, but I was afraid of opening up completely, because I didn't consider the notion of getting close to someone, because the brakes were on for me. However, I couldn't just continue to make small talk with Patrice because I cared for her, loved her, and knew she was unique.

Patrice said, "This is not what is going to take you out. God wouldn't have brought a man as wonderful as you into my life at this time, only to take them away. Let's enjoy the time we have together. If it's a friend you need, I could be your friend. You're not done, and this is not what is going to take you away from me." That moment forever changed our relationship and we became closer and more trusting.

Patrice immediately understood and had compassion for my loss of identity as a surgeon because of my disease, and realized why I was working in TV and living closer to my daughters. As the sun was starting to set, we both shared a tear and talked, and never made it to dinner. I remember kissing her on the cheek goodnight, saying, "I trust you with this secret, and it's hard to trust anyone anymore, because so many of us have been burned." I told her it could cost me my job, because no one wants a "health reporter" who is sick or dying. Patrice was a celebrity in Pittsburgh and I could just imagine how it might affect her if headlines came out saying: *"CBS Medical Correspondent At Death's Door."* I wanted to keep it private, and Patrice understood.

After my diagnosis, I had never wanted to be in a long-term relationship. I didn't think it was fair to the other person, given that I might not be around long. As much as I wanted companionship, I knew what getting married meant. I had not been successful in marriage before, and "long-term" at this point seemed like it could be next month, or maybe a year—definitely not a lifetime. Again, it was almost as if I were always waiting for the other shoe to drop—where a laboratory test result could say that the disease had accelerated. With MDS, once there are some changes that can be found on a simple blood test, by that time (according to some doctors) you are usually "toast."

After I told her about my diagnosis, Patrice tried to learn everything she could about this strange-sounding form of blood/bone cancer—Myelodysplasia (MDS). I know it upset her when I shared some letters from well-known doctors that said I didn't have long to live. This "secret" of my health situation actually brought us closer together and I started to understand a level of love that I hadn't experienced before.

Patrice convinced me that I wasn't going to die anytime soon.

She said she had fallen in love with me, and for selfish reasons (as she put it), she wanted me to stick around for a long time to come. I actually started to believe her, and was not getting ill as frequently as I was in the past. Also, I thought my concoction of supplements and other aspects of the protocol I was using might actually be working (not to make or keep me "young," but simply to help me stay alive.) Still, at the time, I didn't want to allow myself to fall in love with anyone. That part of me couldn't yet open up completely.

Patrice had two wonderful kids from her former marriage, a son Guy and daughter Lauren. At the time I first met them, Lauren was still in high school and Guy was working as an account executive locally in television. Lauren is a beautiful, warm, charming young woman who has great things ahead of her. Guy, when first meeting him, wasn't quite sure about this "Dr. Paul" guy (I sensed) and was extremely protective of his mom, but over time we have grown very close.

I was also very protective of my daughters early on, and didn't immediately introduce them to Patrice. Neither one of us wanted to bring our children into each other's lives too soon. The following May seemed like a good occasion, and Patrice invited me and my daughters to her daughter Lauren's high school graduation party, where she would be celebrating with many of her friends and family. At the graduation party, one of my young daughters said, "Dad, you need to marry her, she's a catch!" As we all got to know one another better, everybody came together. I'm very fortunate that this blended family gets along well.

Telling My Kids

I remember the day I decided to tell my children about my illness. The year was 2005—about six years from my initial diagnosis. When I was first diagnosed in 1999, my daughters were only 9 and 6½ years old— they'd just recently been through the divorce, and were living nearly 700 miles away from their father. I didn't feel it appropriate to tell them at that point. If I wound up being in the hospital a lot, *then and only then* would I discuss it with them. I looked OK, and as far as they knew, Dad just seemed "tired" more than usual. They had no idea how completely exhausted and fatigued I felt on many days.

When Nicole was 15 and Rachael nearly 13, I thought it was time to tell them what was going on with their Dad—why I wasn't actively practicing as a surgeon anymore, and why I was careful about visiting them and others when they had an infection or flu bug of some sort. I drove up to New Castle and picked them up for dinner. Before we arrived at the restaurant, I pulled over into a semi-vacant parking lot, and told them I had something very important to discuss with them. I didn't want their mom (who knew about my illness) to tell them—I wanted it to come from me.

I started the explanation saying, "I have something to tell you about my health." Both of them immediately asked, "Are you going to die, Dad?" I jokingly said, "We're all going to die someday, and I hope I don't 'croak' for a long time—but a number of years ago, the doctors told me I had a type of disease that affected my bone marrow and blood."

I avoided using the word "cancer," and tried to explain in terms they could understand about this strange disease called

MDS. I told them that sometimes my body didn't produce the right type of cells to fight infections. Therefore, I had to stop practicing surgery, because it could expose me to diseases that I might not be able to fight off.

In the simplest terms that I could use, I explained to them that I'd stumbled onto something that was helping me. They knew their Dad had always done lots of research on things, so this was another one of his "projects." I told them I was doing well and feeling pretty good. I also explained that there were some things I couldn't do anymore, like run marathons or even run at all, but I could still take walks with them and be fairly active—although the fatigue and exhaustion that I felt many days was something I didn't discuss.

They both became very quiet. After a few moments, they asked me questions like, "Are you going to be here long?" and "Does it hurt?" As I answered question after question from each daughter, I tried to provide reassurance. I explained to them why I hadn't shared this with them when they were younger. I told them, "All we have on this earth is time—a very precious thing." I always wanted to push to have as much time with them as I could, even though they had many scheduled activities.

Even though I went to as many of their activities as I could—soccer games, recitals, and school functions—I explained that it was very important for us to also have our special dinners and "sleep-overs" every Tuesday night, and our every-other-weekends together at my house. For various reasons, that didn't always work out.

They both wanted to know if my illness was a secret—were they permitted to tell anyone? I told them that it wasn't anything to be ashamed of, but there are some things you don't share openly—you only share with trusted people. I tried to impart a lesson about trust, but also about keeping secrets. Ben Franklin's phrase came to mind—"A secret's good with three people, if two of them are dead." But I smiled and told them that 'no' it wasn't a secret.

Initially they were scared, but over time they realized that I was doing OK and things were back to a "new normal." Everything settled down. The "light bulbs" went on for both of them about why I would fly from Huntsville or LA (or wherever I was) to Pittsburgh to be with them every other weekend.

I wasn't trying to make them fearful of losing their Dad—I was trying to make them understand that time is precious. None of us knows how long we'll be here. The old cliché of "Try to get something meaningful out of each day" rings true. Realize that in the blink of an eye, everything can change. No doubt, these are lessons told from generation to generation. I'm still learning this lesson today—a "work in progress."

Joint Formula 88®

Over the next several years, I continued with my TV gig at KDKA. I also maintained my "protocol" of meds and supplements—although I didn't have the energy I did before the diagnosis, and still had many symptoms, from night sweats and sore throats to just feeling lousy, on many days.

I wasn't seemingly getting any worse, according to some of my doctors. Blood and bone marrow studies seemed to stabilize. Some docs were now saying: "Paul, maybe you're onto something with all these supplements and HGH (Human Growth Hormone) and other things you're taking, especially since you're over six years out from your original 'about two years to live' diagnosis." Yet other docs were skeptical.

What I was doing was very controversial—however, I was no longer just being considered an "outlier," as some docs might say—I was becoming a true miracle, according to some. It went so far as one oncologist telling me, "I still think those supplements and HGH could harm you, BUT I guess go ahead and keep doing it, since you've lived long past what we expected." Not exactly a big vote of confidence from my traditional-allopathic colleagues—anyway, I would take any positive news I could get—and I was still alive.

I was happier to be living closer to my daughters, and having Patrice in my life gave me new strength and purpose. Now that I was beginning to believe I would be around for longer than anticipated, my intellectual curiosity was reignited. I wanted something more.

The HBO (hyperbaric) stuff, where I had been a national expert for years, was no longer a passion as it had once been. The 90-second medical reports I was doing for TV didn't have the depth that I desired. Many times, I felt that critical content, which might actually help people, was being cut for time. "That's just the way TV operates," Patrice explained. She had also warned me, that in very short order I would become bored— knowing my personality.

Was I making any difference in people's lives with these medical reports? It was so unlike the hands-on aspects of being a surgeon that command and demand your full attention during every moment of the surgery. I also missed the relationships I'd built with so many thousands of patients. There was a lot missing with this TV stuff. In my opinion, nothing "holds a candle" to being a surgeon.

One of my personality traits, good or bad, is that I do like immediate feedback. As a surgeon, you frequently know, good or bad, if you've cut the wrong vessel or how a patient is doing. In TV, whether a report made a difference or not, is something you may never find out, although I did receive some kind and thankful letters.

I began to question, "What's the point?"—and "What to do?" Once again, my "idea recliner chair" came through. On a cloudy Pittsburgh day, sitting in the chair where I'd created so many other ideas, I began to think about what else I could do besides the TV stuff. The original idea was hatched back in Huntsville, Alabama in 1988, when I began experimenting and developing a topical pain-relief cream that I thought might help some of my surgical patients. Some of them incidentally had arthritis and muscle aches.

I'd always been interested in doing research on how wounds and how tissue heals, and how to speed up that process. I went on a quest to try to put all my knowledge about pain, tissue, and wound healing into developing a topical pain relief cream. I came up with a rough formula, which I took to some pharmacists and chemists to check out.

The first batch turned out to be a "brown goo" that didn't smell too good. I would hand out small amounts to my patients and ask them to try it, and it seemed to have some efficacy. Years later, I recall my partner and friend, Dr. Jim Garlington saying,

"Nemiroff, I remember you were working on this, because the whole office stunk." Later, I would do further testing to refine the formula, and made sure it was compliant with FDA (Food & Drug Administration) regulations for "over the counter" drugs— lots and lots of testing and paperwork, as you can imagine.

I didn't know back in 1988 what I was really on to—because I was working 80 hours a week and running marathons, I shelved the idea until many years later. It was on that same recliner chair that I decided to pick up where I'd left off, and continue my work on my pain cream. I made dozens of phone calls, spending hundreds of hours doing research on topical pain creams, calling and visiting labs around the country, and finally putting together a formula that I decided to call "Joint Formula 88," because of the early days of working on this cream back in 1988.

The FDA requires you to jump through countless hoops to comply with their rules governing topical pain relief creams. They are quite extensive. Not only did the cream include natural botanicals, but I included real pain-fighting ingredients that had been clinically proven to temporarily relieve pain from arthritis, arthritis-like conditions, muscle aches, strains, and sprains. While it wasn't a "cure" for anything, it could sure knock the pain down. Also, the feedback I was getting from the samples I handed out was extremely positive.

As a surgeon, I knew what an impact pain had on patients. Pain affects every part of someone's life—your personality, your sleep patterns, and your relationships. People who haven't experienced constant pain might not understand. To relieve, or even reduce someone's pain temporarily, was something worth pursuing.

From OR to Entrepreneur—Enter QVC

Once I developed and perfected Joint Formula 88, the next question was—"How do I distribute it to people who might need it?" I didn't know much about retail or "business" in general, and once again began to educate myself about a totally new field. Few doctors make the leap into the business world, and it was not the most familiar territory.

Several business associates suggested that I explore the possibility of selling my Joint Formula 88 on a shopping channel like QVC. I didn't know anything about shopping channels, but Patrice's brother Dave King, was a host there and provided me with some tremendous insights.

I soon discovered that it is extraordinarily difficult to get "on air" at QVC—because of all the jumping through hoops and requirements that they demand. I was also cautioned, by some who'd previously dealt with QVC, that even if I did make it to air, the chances of being successful with this type of product weren't good. Products like this had been on before and hadn't done very well. Living by one of my mottos —"If were easy, then anyone could do it," I decided, "Why not give a try?"

I dug in my heels and was eventually able to get a meeting with a QVC buyer at their headquarters in Westchester, Pennsylvania in 2003. My 10-minute "dog and pony show" didn't go particularly well. The young man said, "Not only will it not work, doc, it's too pricey. We've tried arthritis creams before— even with celebrities as presenters, and it hasn't really worked." Months went by, and I heard nothing.

After dozens of phone calls, emails, and many more hours of effort on my part, QVC finally agreed to give me one 7-minute airing. They ordered 2000 units of Joint Formula 88. The night before I was to go on air, I found out that another pain cream product had recently been on QVC, and had basically flopped—not particularly good news for my pre-airing jitters. It was made clear that there were no guarantees, it was all consignment, and the chances for success were slim—but at least I was getting a chance.

Even though I'd been on TV many times before as a Medical Correspondent, removed bullets from people's necks, and literally dealt with life-and-death situations, I was a nervous wreck before my first airing. I had about five minutes to explain the product to the host, prior to my seven minutes of upcoming airtime later that day. I could feel my heart racing. My mouth was dry and I was thinking, "Can I really do this?"

The moment of truth was upon me. Of course, being colorblind, I never knew which camera to look at, since a red light atop each one signified that it was live, which added to my nervousness. No sooner had I been introduced and started talking for four or five minutes, when the host turned to me and said, "Thank you for being with us," and in the same breath said, "we've just sold out."

I got back to the green room and Patrice was jumping up and down in excitement. Everyone was giving me an "atta-boy." This success was continued with four more "sell-outs" over the months to follow, and one day 20,000 tubes were sold in about 30 minutes of airtime. The numbers were staggering to me.

At the time of this writing, about 11 years after my debut on QVC, I've been on air with several versions of Joint Formula 88 pain relief cream hundreds of times. It continues to surprise everyone with its longevity. The bottom line is that the product works, and is continuing to help people with easing their pain. The letters and testimonials I've received have made it all the more worthwhile. Over a million tubes have been ordered.

The journey at QVC has been a roller coaster. It's a phenomenal place to be involved with, although it has many idiosyncrasies and rules. They do make you jump through a lot of hoops, and I respect them for their close monitoring of people's claims, so that they stand behind their initials QVC—Quality, Value, and Convenience. Make no mistake about it—working with QVC can be fraught with risk for the vendor. Being on for 7 minutes, 10 minutes, or even an hour, is no guarantee you are going to succeed. If you don't continue to hit the required numbers, or "dollars per minute," as they call it—you're gone.

With billions of dollars in sales each year, available in over 90 million households, QVC is an incredible venue if you can get the gig. It's also kind of like being "on call," because sometimes you're given very short notice of when they expect you to be there. If you turn down an airing more than a few times, their response may be— *"Next."*

Some of my doctor friends, as well as others, initially gave me grief about being on QVC—not really knowing why I had gone from surgeon to TV Medical Correspondent to entrepreneur. In fairness, I had kept my medical situation private, and they didn't know the rationale behind my decisions. However, now many of those same doctors and others are coming to me and asking how to get themselves on TV with their "latest greatest product."

Speaks Once

As Patrice and I became closer, I took her somewhere that has always been very special to me, Palm Springs, California—a place which brings back many memories from days as a kid when I went there to the Date Festival. There's an austere beauty of the desert and a true feeling of a healing spiritual ambience. In fact, some of the natural botanicals in Joint Formula 88 were endemic to the Palm Springs area, including one of the components, yucca extract, from a plant that grows wild in that area. The Native American Indians have used yucca extract for a variety of purposes for centuries.

On one of our visits, Patrice and I took a jeep tour with about ten other people to see the San Andreas Fault, and see how the Native Americans lived many years ago. Our tour guide, who was of Native American Indian heritage, knew all the local history. After getting to interact with all of us on the tour, she said she would give each of us an Indian name, based on her first impressions. This custom is followed in her culture, where children are not formally named, sometimes for months, until they have demonstrated some of their personality. She went around the group giving names, such as "Laughing Man" and others. When she got to me, without hesitation (and not knowing anything about me or my professions), she said, "Your name is— SPEAKS ONCE."

Patrice thought this name was very appropriate for me. She said that whenever I walked into a room, I had some form of presence, and my voice affected people in a positive way. As a surgeon in the OR, I rarely had to repeat myself more than once. To this day, when I've made some sort of decisive comment,

Patrice will jokingly say "OK, Speaks Once." (Unless, of course, it has to do with helping out with the household chores.)

As friendship and trust bloomed into romance, I eventually asked Patrice to marry me, something neither she nor I thought we would do again. Her warmth and compassion, and the fact that she is an incredible mom to her two kids, were all things that attracted me to her. Of course, her natural beauty didn't hurt. Most importantly, I felt a special connection to her unlike anything I'd experienced before. I guess I was learning the true meaning of what love was all about.

I proposed to Patrice in Chicago, coincidentally at an Anti-Aging Conference. Perhaps it was an appropriate place to tell another person, "I want to grow old with you." I had wanted to propose to her in Palm Springs the week before, but the time was never quite right. Although we had dated for several years, we hadn't discussed marriage to that point. I had flowers sent up to the room, along with chocolate dipped strawberries. I did the getting down on "one knee" thing because it just felt like the right thing to do—and she said yes.

We were engaged for about a year and then had a wonderful intimate marriage ceremony in the Palm Springs area in July 2007. My daughters Nicole and Rachael "gave me away." I feel incredibly lucky to have her as my wife and to have a wonderful blended family where people actually like each other. Patrice's Mom, Dee, her brothers Brett and Dave, and her two children Lauren and Guy have become cherished members of my family.

with Patrice in Palm Springs

Random Acts of Kindness

What if longevity was somehow linked to how useful we are or how kind we treat others—that is, as long as we're beneficial to others, we get to stick around. It's a naïve notion, I know, considering all the random death in the world. Nevertheless, the idea has crossed my mind on more than occasion as I've become more conscious of my own mortality.

I have tried to be the best father I can to my daughters, although I know I haven't been perfect. And I believe I've been a positive force in the lives of Patrice and her children, as well as people in the newsroom, and many others who have sought my advice and assistance as a physician. I've even had the privilege of saving a few lives since leaving the practice of medicine. One such event occurred on January 17th, 2006.

I'd just arrived at Pittsburgh Airport where I was meeting Patrice to travel to Palm Springs. I was running about 10 minutes late, unusual for me, so I was feeling a bit frantic. Patrice and I checked in at US Airways and we were taking our baggage to be checked in at security. As we were checking our luggage, out of the corner of my eye I noticed a man who looked like a piece of timber falling to the floor. In mid-conversation, I jumped over the security ropes and ran toward him to see if I could help.

The man lay motionless on the floor with blood all over his face. I quickly turned him over and took his pulse, and there wasn't one. He was turning blue. Assessing that he had a cardiac arrest, I began CPR and started calling out for an "AED" (Automated External Defibrillator)—these are often found in airports, but no one knew what I was talking about. Patrice explained, "He needs a defibrillator!"

I ripped open the man's shirt, thumped his chest with some force, and continued CPR. After asking his wife what his name was, I shouted at the man, "Come on Jim, stay with me." Police, security people, and a large crowd quickly surrounded us. Patrice, who is a well-known public figure particularly in Pittsburgh, assured the gathering crowd of on lookers, especially some that recognized me from TV, that I was in fact a "real doctor"—not just "playing one on TV."

Patrice was right there, watching me thump the poor man's chest, and put her arm around the man's wife to console her, offering her a bottle of water and some support. Then the woman said, "Are you Patrice from TV?" "Yes," Patrice answered, "and that's Dr. Paul—your husband is in good hands." I couldn't have asked for a better assistant. Someone finally brought a defibrillator, just as a paramedic team arrived, and we all worked together to save Jim's life. He regained a pulse, and although he still had irregular heartbeats, he was back from the brink and en route to the hospital.

Patrice and I thought we had missed our plane. Then, to our surprise, we learned that US Airways had literally held the plane for us for an extra hour. Can you believe that? Since this was the last flight of the day to LA, we were grateful. When we arrived in LA, I called the hospital to make sure Jim was okay. I spoke with his family several times to try to answer questions and generally just be supportive. Jim Jenkins remained in a coma for several days, waking up just in time for the Pittsburgh Steelers AFC championship game. The story of his rescue by "Dr. Paul" ran in *The Pittsburgh Post Gazette* under the title: *"Random Acts of Kindness."*

This was a first for Patrice—she had never seen me in action. I remember her saying to me, "There is nothing you could ever do that is going to surpass that. You held that man's life in your hands." Wow, I really missed being a practicing surgeon.

Mr. Jenkins still writes us every year on the anniversary of his rescue. Every Christmas, he sends us one sort of goodie or another. He insisted on writing me a check for saving his life, which I refused to accept—finally, I suggested he write a check to the MDS Foundation, which he did. As of this writing, Jim's doing fine.

I later got a call from a staff member at the MDS Foundation as well as from the head of the Foundation, Dr. Bennett, who years earlier had confirmed my MDS diagnosis and stage, asking if they could release the information—that I actually had MDS— as part of the story. I replied, "No. Just say that Mr. Jenkins donated the money—I don't want the information on my illness out." It was still my secret.

Act of Kindness

Recently we received a wonderful letter from Chris Jenkins detailing the events of Tuesday, January 17, 2006 when Dr. Paul Nemiroff saved the life of his father, Jim Jenkins at the Pittsburgh International Airport.

As his father lay dying from a heart attack, Dr. Nemiroff sprang into action and kept him alive until the paramedics arrived. Without his gallant efforts, Chris feels his father would not be here today. Furthermore, when his family expressed a desire to repay him in some way, he graciously suggested that they make a donation to our Foundation.

The MDS Foundation would like to acknowledge Paul Nemiroff's heroism and we feel he should be recognized for his courageous act of kindness and commitment to helping the Foundation.

Dr. Nemiroff is a nationally recognized surgeon, television medical correspondent, winner of the prestigious 2003 C. Everett Koop Surgeon General Media Award, presented by the American Heart Association, and author of over 100 articles and research papers in the medical sciences.

MDS Foundation Newsletter—Winter 2006

Overstepping Boundaries

During that same month as I helped Mr. Jenkins in 2006, the Sago Mine explosion occurred. The terrible blast trapped 13 West Virginia miners for nearly two days. Patrice was live on the air, reporting the story as it unfolded, when the newsroom got word from CNN that 12 of the 13 miners had miraculously survived. That's what the wire services were reporting, and CNN announced it on the air. Patrice followed with a similar announcement, saying that it was unconfirmed, but according to sources, 12 miners had been found alive.

Then, a half-hour later, someone slipped Patrice a note saying: "WRONG INFORMATION. ALL DEAD BUT ONE." The miscommunication, it turned out, had occurred between the rescue workers down in the mine and the command center at the surface, where company and state officials, as well as representatives from the governor's office, were present.

"I was thinking," Patrice recalls, "how can I do this as gently as possible and tell everyone what really has happened. So I got on the air and said, 'I can't believe I have to tell you this, but there has been a horrible mistake. We have in fact confirmed that only one miner is alive.'"

It was at that point that Patrice called me at home. I had been doing live interviews over the phone, answering questions about survivability, how long people can live in such a situation without oxygen, and how long before carbon monoxide poisoning sets in.

When Patrice told me that only one miner had survived, my response was, "That miner needs hyperbaric oxygen immediately." He had been down there for two days and I believed he was suffering from carbon monoxide poisoning. That night, I contacted the emergency room at the local hospital where the miner had been taken and learned that the man was in a coma. I told them that they should test the carbon monoxide levels in his blood, and maybe treat him with hyperbaric oxygen. I explained who I was, and that I was an expert in HBO.

The physician in charge said he'd look into it. The next morning I called again and got the same ER guy. "Did you run a carboxyhemoglobin on him?" I asked.

"Well, he's in a coma," he said. "He's not responsive."

"I know," I said, "but did you run the test?" Reportedly he hadn't, or wasn't sure.

I suggested that since the other miners had died from carbon monoxide poisoning that they just go ahead and treat him with hyperbaric oxygen anyway.

"We'll just treat him with regular oxygen," the ER guy said.

I replied, "In my opinion, I think you're making a mistake. Why not try HBO? You've got nothing to lose."

"Well," he said, "he's essentially dead. There's very little brain activity." It was useless.

The next day the man was still alive—so I called again. This time I told the doctor that I was with CBS television, but that I was also a surgeon and known nationally as an expert in hyperbaric oxygen—and just wanted to help. "It could actually bring him around," I said. "I've seen it bring back coma victims before."

"Well," he replied, "we don't have a chamber here."

I was really getting frustrated. I was essentially dealing with a small town hospital with little understanding of the value of hyperbaric oxygen. When I called the next day, I learned they had shipped the miner to a hospital in West Virginia that also didn't have a chamber. This time, I got the head of the internal medicine program, who was an ER doc, and he listened. He also recognized my name as an HBO expert.

"Do you really think the guy might wake up at this late date?"

"Yes," I said. "I've seen coma cases where the patient is essentially dead and they wake up. I've treated thousands of patients with HBO. But you're running out of time. You need to transfer him to the closest HBO unit right away. There's nothing to lose."

Finally, I called Allegheny General Hospital in Pittsburgh, where they had an HBO chamber, and put them in touch with the doctor at the other hospital. The patient was shipped over by ambulance and put immediately into the chamber. Lo and behold—after the first two-hour treatment, the man started to wake up. Everybody was calling it a miracle.

With continued treatments, the man made a recovery. He reportedly had some brain damage and wasn't perfect, but with physical therapy, he was able to return to his family and still have a life. I had sort of overstepped my boundaries, but it was worth it. I didn't want any credit—I wasn't the treating physician—but it felt great to have played a part in saving this man's life. Being able to make a difference in people's lives was very important to me—always knowing that I still couldn't actively practice surgery and medicine because of exposure to infections—could cost me my life.

White House Calling

Patrice and I were in Santa Monica, California, where we had taken one of my daughters, Nicole and several of her teenage girl friends for her birthday. It was a Friday afternoon, June 26th, 2009. The two of us, having left the girls to their own devices on the beach, were walking from our hotel in the direction of the Santa Monica Pier. The two of us laughed as we thought of the four bathing beauties we'd left on the beach, who were glad we were with them—but not that glad.

I didn't even hear my cell phone ring. It wasn't until a couple of minutes later, when it vibrated, signaling a voice message, that I checked it. The caller ID read a 202 number—Washington, D.C. I couldn't think of anyone in Washington who would be calling me. I would have let it go, but my curiosity got the better of me.

What I heard when I dialed in was something I will never forget.

"What is it?" Patrice said.

"Just a minute," I told her as I listened to the last of the message. "Just a minute."

I saved the message and played it back on speakerphone. We just stood there mesmerized. It went something like this:

"Dr. Nemiroff, I'm the Director of Presidential Personnel at the White House. We are aware of your impressive credentials and would very much like to speak with you about a "position" in the Administration. Please call me as soon as possible." He had given me the number for his assistant—then, after hesitating for a moment he said, "Let me give you my direct number also."

Patrice and I just stood there with our mouths agape as I played it back a couple of times. "Oh, my Goodness." Patrice finally said.

"I know," I said. "This is serious if he's giving his direct number. I'd better call him right now." But it was too late—they had already left for the day. It was Friday, which meant we'd have to wait until Monday to call back. It was going to be a long weekend. Neither of us knew for certain what this out-of-the-blue White House call was about, and yet we had an idea. We just weren't expecting it—not in our wildest dreams.

The whole thing started a couple of months earlier when we were flying back from one of our weekends in Palm Springs. While Patrice was reading her book—it's the only time she can set aside time for reading—I was talking to the gentleman sitting on the other side of me, a judge from Pittsburgh involved in national politics. We knew some people in common, and before long we were sharing our life stories. The discussion eventually turned to health care, and the pending appointment of a new US Surgeon General by the Obama Administration.

It was at that point that Patrice, having joined the conversation, came right out and said, "Paul would make a great Surgeon General."

Whenever I started talking about healthcare issues, Patrice would say, "You'd be good for the country. First of all, you really care. You've got the administrative mind, the experience in many aspects of healthcare, and you're a terrific communicator. You'd be great." This time, her remark seemed to hit a chord with the judge.

"I think you're right," he said. "I can tell just from talking to him, and with his credentials, he would make a great Surgeon General." We didn't think much about the conversation on the plane, until surprisingly, a few weeks later—things started to happen that, based on that conversation, were pretty incredible.

A series of phone calls with US Senators and their Chiefs of Staff, background checks, and vetting procedures ensued. Eventually I was asked to come to Washington, D.C. for an interview as a candidate for Surgeon General of the United States.

My day at the White House was set in July 2009. Without telling anyone where she was going, Patrice took a couple of days off from the newsroom and the two of us got into the car and drove the four hours from Pittsburgh to Washington for our appointment at the White House. And we figured we'd get in a little sightseeing—Patrice was determined to show me the Lincoln Monument at dusk.

We had dinner in Georgetown that night near our hotel. The next morning we took a cab to the White House, arriving 45 minutes early, as instructed. After passing through three layers of metal detectors and having our passports and other forms of identification checked and rechecked by various security personnel, we finally found ourselves sitting in a small waiting room outside the office of the Director of Presidential Personnel.

It was a great meeting—scheduled for only 20 minutes, but lasting nearly two and half hours. I was quizzed and grilled on everything from current health care issues to whether had I paid all my taxes—and did I ever have an "undocumented" nanny— so many questions. Finally, at one point I was told: "The

President is aware of you Dr. Nemiroff, and you are on the short list for US Surgeon General, the very short list." Wow, that was nice to know.

It was all very exciting—coupled with having been able to "touch" the desk of President John F. Kennedy while in one of the Senators' offices, was awe-inspiring. And the Lincoln Memorial at dusk was all Patrice said it would be. Perhaps I was going to be able to serve and make a difference. But it was not to be—I didn't get the gig.

I've been told, "Favor isn't always YES." While initially very disappointed, I look back now and believe I may have "dodged a bullet"—given all the recent acrimony about health care. "And the beat goes on."

15

QUEST FOR A CURE

So I didn't get the White House gig. I went back to Pittsburgh and continued my research on anti-oxidants and nutritional supplements, while still doing TV work writing and presenting medical information. To the surprise of all my doctors and myself, my medical condition remained fairly stable over the years, with routine blood tests, bone marrow biopsies and doctor visits—but again, only a couple of friends and family members knew, because I appeared relatively healthy.

Still there was a "new normal" for me—not being able to run or exercise like I had before, or have even half the energy I had prior to being diagnosed—but I was thankful to still be functioning reasonably well—all the while being supported by my wife Patrice, and continuing my relationships with all our kids and family. But again there was, with the rest of the world, a double life—in a sense. No one really knew why I retired from being a surgeon—most of the world did not know I was "terminally ill."

I wanted my privacy and really didn't want to share this

"secret" with anyone. It was just too painful to relive each detail, and it can, at least with some people, change their perceptions of you. Also, it wasn't anyone's business—it was my choice to disclose the situation or not.

Just when I became restless and wanted to do more meaningful projects with health care and nutritional supplements, a friend with whom I worked on previous projects, Charlie Amidon, a former instructor of Navy Seals, called me.

"Hey Doc, it's Charlie. What do you know about Enzymes?"

"Well Charlie, I know something about enzymes—but what kind are you talking about?"

"Well, how 'bout I come to Pittsburgh and take you and Patrice to dinner this Thursday and tell you all about it?"

"Sure Charlie, see you then."

The day he planned to visit was November 9th, 2010—nearly 11 years out from the fateful call of November 18th, 1999. I really didn't know what Charlie was up to—but what I did know, and still know, that he is one guy that if I were ever in a war, or a super tight spot, I'd want him fighting alongside me in the foxhole.

After a wonderful dinner, Charlie explained that he was the new CFO for a company near Branson, Missouri called National Enzyme Company. They specialize in producing nutritional supplements and especially enzymes, which support and can optimize digestive processes.

Charlie wanted me to meet the owner and CEO—Tony Collier, who is passionate about digestive enzymes and also a very kind and generous man. When I traveled to Branson,

Missouri to meet with Tony, Charlie, and other staffers, they asked me if I would be interested in doing some research for them on digestive enzymes.

"Sure," I said.

Thus began a great working relationship with NEC, including many travels to their Forsyth headquarters. As I poured over the research on enzymes—of which there are many types—I realized that my medical school training gave little if any discussion on how these powerful substances—"life forces" that they are— could help support one's immune system, digestive tract, and be involved in virtually every chemical reaction in the body. I was astounded. Why hadn't I heard much about "enzyme therapy" before?

Part of it is the medical dogma that still lies in the traditional medical field training—with resistance to change, and being very cautious. I had faced this before with my hyperbaric oxygen work. The other part of it was simply that most American doctors had no exposure to enzyme therapy, as do doctors in many other parts of the world.

An entire new adventure for me was about to begin—not only doing research and getting the word out about enzymes and nutritional supplements, but adding daily digestive enzymes to my own protocol. Soon, I noted that my gastric distress had vanished, as long as I took a couple of these digestive enzymes along with my meals. No longer did I ask my wife to buy me the big bottles of the H2 blockers—you know, the kind that helps block stomach acid—but also has other side effects. Bottom line—my tummy felt better.

Melted Candle

It was a warm spring day in April 2011 in Missouri. I'd finished doing some consulting work with National Enzyme Company, and was heading back to my hotel. I noticed that my right eye was watering for some reason. Maybe it was because it was a windy day, or the pollen count was up? I went to bed around 10 p.m. only to awaken around 2 a.m.—instinctively, I knew something was wrong with my eye and face—I couldn't whistle. As a doc, I instinctively knew this could be a problem—meaning that some of the muscles of my face were not working right.

I stumbled to turn on a light then looked in the mirror, only to see the right side of my face drooping. I let out an (expletive deleted) and quickly realized what was wrong. It wasn't a stroke—it was Bell's palsy, a paralyzing of the facial nerve that feeds the various muscles that move the face.

I had treated many patients over the years for this problem and realized that about 80-85% of the time things get better and the patient recovers. However, about 15-20% of the time, patients don't recover—or they at least have severe residual problems—like not being able to smile or show expression on one side of their face, or worse—like having problems even talking.

"Wow," I thought—this isn't particularly good. I found a Band-Aid® in my shaving kit and put it over my right eye to keep it closed. One of the problems with Bell's palsy is that your eye won't close and can quickly become dry, and then infected. Part of the treatment for Bell's is eye protection—which can include various creams, drops and other goops, as well as a patch.

I went to bed, knowing that I would be heading to a pharmacy as soon as one opened, to get some of the standard medications that may help in the case of Bell's—while also planning to catch a flight home to see a specialist. In the morning, the pharmacist filled a prescription for heavy dose steroids (prednisone) that's thought to help in some cases, as well as an anti-viral agent that some doctors think may help. I began taking them at once and headed back to Pittsburgh.

It was about two days later when I got into see the specialist at the University of Pittsburgh—a good doc, head of their neuro-otology department, which deals with this condition. After some tests, he agreed with my diagnosis and recommended we watch things closely and see how things progress. I was on all the right meds, and hopefully things would improve over the next few weeks.

Well, knowing "way too much" about this entity, coupled with the fact that I was having tremendous pain behind my ear and had a host of horrible side-effects from the medications, I insisted on some additional tests to assess how the facial nerve (cranial nerve 7) was doing. Was it getting better, or was it dying?

Too all of our chagrin, things kept getting worse and I was running out of time now—since you have about 10 days to two weeks to decide on a very tricky, risky brain surgery, that many times does not work. My face was deteriorating like a "melted candle"—my wife later told me—and the pain became horrific. It was no surprise to hear that my facial nerve was dying quickly—roughly 75% of it was on its way out.

The doctor at the hospital knew my background and knew that I had been involved with the type of brain surgery which removes pressure around the nerve. I told him I wasn't interested and would take my chances—and that I was starting experimental hyperbaric oxygen treatments, as well as taking several enzyme supplements—all with a goal of reducing inflammation and swelling around my ever-dying facial nerve. Research in Europe and other parts of the world have shown that certain enzyme supplements appear to reduce inflammation. I thought of a two pronged approach on reducing some of the pressure off my facial nerve—one of the theories of what causes Bell's palsy—by using both HBO and enzyme therapy.

Of course, no great trials had been done with HBO and facial nerve paralysis but then again, I was an "expert" in the field of hyperbaric medicine, and based on some of its mechanisms of action—by bringing more oxygen, and reducing swelling, I thought, "What have I got to lose?"

Also, the prospect of having permanent paralysis of my face was not particularly comforting. While a high percentage of people do recover from Bell's, it all depends on their stage of the problem—which ranges from 1 to 6—with 6 being the very worst—I was a 6+. Nothing worked on the right side of my face—drooling, looking like I'd had a stroke, a metallic taste on part of my tongue, unable to drink from a glass without liquid pouring all over me, wearing a black eye patch and using ointment continually for my eye, and prospects of even needing special eye surgery, plus horrible pain. I thought, "Well, there go my speaking and TV careers"—another obstacle to overcome.

Because of having worked in the field of HBO for so long, most of the hyperbaric chamber facilities had heard of me—they even had a book on HBO that I helped author—so I was able to start treatments immediately, realizing that insurance might not pay for it, but figured I'd work out the payments later. Time was running out.

Patrice drove me virtually every day over the next month for 30 two-hour HBO treatments. She'd patiently drive the one hour to get me there, then wait while the treatment proceeded, then drive me home—an emotionally exhausting day for both of us.

Almost magically, after the first couple of treatments, I noticed the pain behind my ear started to go down—but of course my face was still completely, and I mean completely, paralyzed. Over the course of another week or so of treatment, small spontaneous movements would occur, almost as if the nerve in my face was struggling to arise. Slowly, over the next month, it did—with virtually full return. I'd gone from a level 6 back to "normal"—as normal as my face looks usually. It really was amazing—I had my face back, and my life. Another bullet dodged—perhaps another of my nine lives used up?

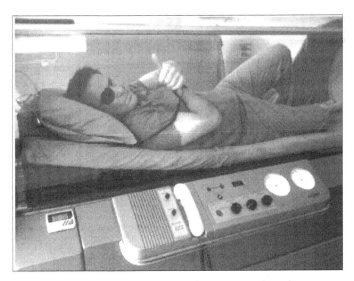

Recovering in a hyperbaric oxygen chamber

The doctor was amazed and rounded up all his residents to see a "miracle." The doc was so astounded that he suggested we publish the case. When diagnosed with an illness or when facing the problem—try to think outside the box. You can feel sorry for yourself for a while—and I guess it's part of the grieving process—but you have to keep getting back up and figure out a way to overcome the obstacles. If not, you may have to start getting used to a "new normal," and don't want to be in the role of "victim" for long. I don't necessarily recommend this treatment for everyone—always check with your doctor—all I can say is that it worked for me, and I'd do it again in a heartbeat.

Rate of Acceleration

Another year passed—now I was 12 years out from my MDS diagnosis—doing reasonably well—and then on a routine PSA testing (prostate antigen for cancer—a blood test), another non-welcome surprise. Over the last year, my PSA had been rising—not excessively high (just over 4), but it had gone up fairly rapidly from a 2. Although fraught with controversy, the PSA test does have its value, especially when the "rate of acceleration," or rate of change, occurs rather quickly.

After a few more blood tests to confirm the diagnosis, I got a prostate "ultrasound" guided biopsy. Of course, I'm taking all the antibiotics pre and post op—as well as some doses of my prescription white cell blood booster. The good news—no cancer. The bad news—about 48 hours after the biopsy, I became extremely weak, with a skyrocketing fever, and was rushed by ambulance to the hospital. I knew what was wrong—I was septic (through no fault of any of the docs). My body didn't handle the biopsies in the prostate well, and bacteria swept through my blood stream. Maybe the MDS was going to win out after all?

A week in the hospital with numerous life-saving IV antibiotics and other treatments brought me around. I lost 20 lbs. in 10 days. Friends jokingly said, "Gee, you look great—which diet were you on?" I replied, "One you don't want to try." Or, as Patrice said tongue-in-cheek said, "Hey, you almost died, but you look great—most women would kill to lose 20 lbs. so fast." It was another wake up call—another of my nine lives—time to focus on doing only what you want most, and not doing what you don't want.

Patrice had been on the air for nearly 33 years—anchoring the 4 p.m., 6 p.m., and 11 p.m. news in Pittsburgh. News and TV had changed so much, not for the better, and she was ready to move on—coupled with the fact that our kids were all out of the house, either working or in college. We both decided a change was needed. I'd been in Pittsburgh about a decade and longed for the warm bright sunny skies of California. The thought of another brutal Pittsburgh winter was overwhelming.

Patrice, with a huge send-out from her friends, family, and hundreds of thousands of viewers, finally said her "goodbyes" on air that year—a performance watched and re-watched 1000s of times on the websites—it was time to go. Just before leaving Pittsburgh, Patrice won a Lifetime Achievement Emmy Award for broadcasting—the culmination of over three decades of TV talk and news—having interviewed world famous celebrities, movie stars, sports figures, as well as presidents and first ladies. The little girl from Sheraton, Pennsylvania and the boy from East LA were headed west.

California Here We Come

We moved to a gorgeous area of the country—Laguna Niguel—located a few miles from the Pacific Ocean, with near perfect weather year round. Patrice continued doing TV work and voice-over projects, and I continued with my research on life-changing supplements, consulting, and lecturing to various healthcare professionals. Still, only a handful of people knew about my ticking time bomb.

One evening we returned from a walk along a path outside our home, having just watched a beautiful sunset. Patrice and I were at feeling at peace. You know there's a saying that there are times in your life that everything seem just right—you feel healthy, your kids are OK, you aren't destitute and can pay your bills, and life seems great. Well, it turned out it was not one of those times—again.

When we returned home, there was a phone message from one of my docs saying we needed to talk. Oh no. I called the doctor back and asked, "Is there some change in my MDS status?"

"No," he replied, "but your recent blood tests show a disturbing rise in your PSA—now it's 9.7—you need another biopsy."

"No," I said, "I'm not having any more regular type biopsies—the last one almost did me in."

"Well," he said, "we can 'follow' it for a while."

This wasn't particularly comforting—since I "knew too much." While PSAs are very controversial, a rising one is not usually a good thing. It doesn't always mean cancer—it's either that, or it could possibly be an infection, or other things. Also, your prostate grows as you age and can cause a rise in your PSA.

I embarked on research of the "latest greatest" ways to diagnose and confirm prostate cancer, and with ways to reduce my risk of the tests and treatment being worse than the disease itself. I discovered a team of docs doing something called "MRI-guided needle biopsy of the prostate"—incredibly accurate, and in my case, we could just do the scan and see what was up, without necessarily needing a biopsy. I had the test, along with some IV antibiotics—feeling great anticipation and worry as I awaited results. The "what-ifs" continued—was this going to be it?

The scan showed some highly suspicious areas, and coupled with my rising PSA, and under the care of several docs—proceeded with the MRI directed biopsies. I did fine—no sepsis this time—but again, the waiting for results was agonizing. For those docs who decide to have their nurses or assistants call patients on a Friday and leave a message on their voicemail—please don't. Anything should be discussed in person, or at least "in person" on the phone.

Patrice and I once again were walking outside on that beautiful trail. She came home sooner to start dinner, and when I returned, she told me she had read the email—directed to both of us. She was smiling and exuberant—she had read the results and she said there was no cancer—"Thank God—I get to keep my Paul!"

Then the other shoe dropped. Patrice had read the first page of the report, however the attachment contained ominous news—**very aggressive type prostate cancer** in several areas of the prostate. The tears of joy turned from happiness to disbelief—for both of us—now what?

Once again, I began searching for answers and asking the right questions. Although I'm a physician and surgeon, every area of medicine has its uniqueness and specifics—no one can be an expert in every area, but I was going to try. The doctors and hospital visits, the tests, and the potential complications were overwhelming. Given my unique situation with MDS and prostate cancer, I asked myself, "What is the best treatment and best chances for survival?"

On one of my doctor visits I decided to check out City of Hope—one of the hospitals that I consulted with when I was first diagnosed with MDS some 14 years earlier. They had recommended an eventual bone marrow transplant for me, which I'd declined. After seeing the surgeon there, a guy who had done 2500 of these types of cases, and who had an excellent reputation, he indicated that I would need to see an oncologist, an infectious disease doctor, and others to decide whether or not my body could even "handle" a long delicate surgical procedure, given my MDS.

NATIONAL MEDICAL CENTER AND
BECKMAN RESEARCH INSTITUTE

Where the Power of Knowledge Saves Lives™

Stephen J. Forman, M.D., F.A.C.P.
Director

David S. Snyder, M.D., F.A.C.P.
Associate Director

Auayporn P. Nademanee, M.D.
Associate Clinical Director
Director, Unrelated Donor BMT Program

Margaret R. O'Donnell, M.D., F.R.C.P.C.
Associate Clinical Director

Pablo Parker, M.D.
Anthony Stein, M.D.
J.R. Wong, Jr., M.D.
Kim A. Margolin, M.D., F.A.C.P.
George Somlo, M.D., F.A.C.P.
Warren A. Chow, M.D.
Henry C. Fung, M.D., F.R.C.P.E.
Ravi Bhatia, M.D.
Amrita Krishnan, M.D.
Robert Rodriguez, M.D.
Leslie Popplewell, M.D.
Jasmine Zain, M.D.
Ryotaro Nakamura, M.D.
Mark Kirschbaum, M.D.
Karen Aboody, M.D.
Mark V. McNamara, M.D.
Don J. Diamond, Ph.D.
Chu-Chih Shih, Ph.D.
Lynn Bowers, N.P.
Barbara Srehn, PA-C
Rose Movsesahl, PA-C
Linda Mangan, PA-C

Fellows
Zaid Al-Kadhimi, M.D.
Vinod Pullarkar, M.D.
Maria Angelopoulou, M.D.

Pediatric BMT
Joseph Rosenthal, M.D.
Director

Robert Sweetman, M.D.
Smita Bhatia, M.D., M.P.H.
Michael C.V. Jensen, M.D.
Laurence Cooper, M.D.

Stem Cell Biology Program
Ravi Bhatia, M.D.
Director

Center for Applied Biomedicine & Genetics
David DiGiusto, Ph.D.
Manager

City of Hope • Samaritan Transplant Program-Phoenix
Jeffrey R. Schriber, M.D., F.R.C.P.
Director

Joseph C. Alvarnas, M.D.
Director, Cell Processing
Clarence Sarkodee-Adoo, M.D.

City of Hope • Kaiser Permanente
Peter M. Falk, M.D., Co-Director
Neil M. Kogut, M.D., Co-Director
Firoozeh Sahebi, M.D.
Ricardo T. Spielberger, M.D.

HLA Laboratory
David Senitzer, Ph.D.
Director

Unrelated BMT Program Coordinator
Jean Blaylock, R.N., B.S.N.
Kathy Neves, R.N.
Fax: (626) 301-8348

Professional Practice Leader
Sharon Steingass

Nurse Coordinators
Mei Cheung, R.N.
Holly Kinahan, R.N.
Emily Krupka, R.N.
Kathryn Penne, R.N.
Allison Seno, R.N.
Debra Vasquez, R.N.

Administrative Director
Gail K. Herndon, M.B.A.

Division of Hematology and
Bone Marrow Transplantation

July 28, 2003

Paul Nemiroff, M.D.

Dear Dr. Nemiroff:

You visited City of Hope in January of 2000 seeking a second opinion regarding your diagnosis of Myelodysplastic Syndrome. At that time it was recommended that bone marrow transplantation be done and a Matched Unrelated Donor search was initiated. It has been some time since we have heard from you. Do you still wish our center to continue coordinating a matched unrelated donor search on your behalf? If so, would you ask your hematologist to send us copies of any recent labs, marrow results and updates on your progress.

We look forward to hearing from you soon. Please let us know if you have any questions.

Sincerely,

Margaret O'Donnell, M.D.
Division of Hematology and
Bone Marrow Transplantation

MRO'D/bg

1500 East Duarte Road, Duarte, CA 91010-3000

A National Cancer Institute-designated Comprehensive Cancer Center

Given my episode with sepsis, and my white cell count that wasn't normal, and the cells themselves didn't fight infection very well—he wasn't sure. I met with an ID doc, then an Oncologist/Hematologist—and there was Dr. Margaret O'Donnell—14 years later—extraordinarily surprised and pleased that I was still alive—recalling the letter I received from her about my January 2000 visit when she recommended a bone marrow transplant.

We both laughed and I said, "Glad I didn't try the bone marrow transplant—I'm certain I wouldn't have made it." Dr. O'Donnell smiled and said, "I'm glad you didn't either—and you're still here. Remarkable—what have you been doing to stay so well?"

I filled her in on my protocol of supplements, HGH, and testosterone, and she said, "Well that's great—you clearly still have MDS, but somehow you're one of the extremely rare patients to have made it this long—but now you face another major challenge. Let me put together a 'battle plan' with several doctors and we'll all make a decision as to whether we think you can handle the operation."

Of course, my other oncologists thought that I was much more than just a "rarity" when it came to survival—they thought it was a miracle I'd made it this long. Being a surgeon, and after doing much research on it, I had decided that my best long-term survival was with surgery—if I could make it off the OR table.

After considering all sorts of options and getting the belief from all the docs that they could all monitor me carefully and thought that I had a "reasonable chance" of surviving, and not becoming septic—I eventually decided on robotic surgery. There was so much preparation for the surgery—with tests, and more tests. The anticipation and "not knowing" are the hardest, not just for the patient, but the family. Patrice was there for me every step of the way.

I had the benefit of being a physician and surgeon—but I would still strongly recommend anyone facing this situation to educate themselves the best they can by reading books or articles on the topic, and getting second, and even third opinions in some cases. Medicine isn't an exact science. For example, at the turn of the last century (1890s), pharmaceutical company Bayer® reportedly said they had found a cure for opium addiction—drum roll…..it was heroin! So much for medicine being an "exact science."

Time Stands Still

I thought, "Wow, we had just recently moved to California—and now all of it might be over?" Time seemed to stand still—the countdown to surgery continued—getting all of one's affairs in order, talking with kids and family, and then wondering and worrying about the "what ifs." Sometimes ignorance is bliss— knowing about all the other risks and complications, especially in my situation, gave me great pause. I was tired, and began to question: "To Be, or Not To Be." Around this time, I had a phone conversation with my good friend Dr. Dexter (Dex) Blome. He followed up with an email to me in October 2013 saying:

"Nem—I know that this is such a difficult time and, obviously, agonizing for you both. You've had a great 14-year run, but, my

friend, that was just the prelude for the next 14 years. You have astounded everyone, including yourself, and I feel quite confident that you'll keep doing so for many, many years to come. As we've talked about, the Nem has nine lives and has only used up seven. (How we arrived at that number, I don't know, but it sounds reasonable.) Anyway, you've got at least two more, so go for it."

Without question you're in a daunting and frightening place right now, but you are one hell of a strong person, and have no doubt researched every angle of possible treatment, result, risk and complication. I have no doubt that your final decision will be the most appropriate and the best. I feel certain that YOU WILL COME OUT OF THIS LANDING ON YOUR FEET—as the Nem always does.

You're a very special person who has accomplished more in 60% of your life than any other 5 people could accomplish in their entire lives. Now, you've got at least 40% left to double your previous successes—get busy living. Besides, that VERY YOUNG, vivacious, accomplished and attractive woman that you married needs you to stick around. You guys make a phenomenal looking couple, but honestly, no one's looking at you—as Patrice is the real attraction. You really did marry over your head, Nem. Anyway, forgive my ramblings, but it's late here and old guys like me tend to go on and on and on when tired.

Have a good night, my friend and know that you've got a lot of people that love you.

Dex

This letter was a tremendous spirit booster for me and frankly gave me additional strength to push on. Meanwhile, Patrice was "dancing as fast as she could," as she likes to say, and wanted to know what I might want to do before the "big day." I told her that I thought we should have some laughs together. "Let's go see your pal Dennis Miller in Las Vegas."

Patrice and Dennis had known each other for nearly 30 years—he used to open for Patrice's talk show in Pittsburgh. His show had long been sold out, so Patrice called Dennis. "Hey Den, we were really trying to come see you but apparently some other folks had the same idea—any pull on getting some tickets?"

"P," as Dennis always called her, "magically" got us two incredible seats, and we had a chance to visit with him alone in the green room before the show. He was very gracious and funny, and said a prayer for Patrice and me for the upcoming surgery.

We returned from Las Vegas and the next week headed for pre-op and more tests before the "big day"—which was initially supposed to be on November 18th—but I didn't like the "vibe"—and it turned out to be about a week "after" my 14th year of survival since my MDS diagnosis.

I made it through the surgery, although I had some complications. For a time, it was a rough road. The best news was that the cancer had been "over-staged" to a degree—which sometimes happens, as surgeons don't really know the extent until it's "in a bucket" in the pathology office—and I was cancer free. Of all the lymph nodes, none were positive, and all the surgical margins were clear. Follow-up visits have shown that I'm cancer free, at least with respect to the prostate cancer. MDS is unfortunately still in my body—but it's not taking me out.

Work in Progress

During my recuperation period, I knew it was time to get my story on paper, recalling the line from the movie *The Shawshank Redemption:* "You'd better get busy living, or get busy dying." For many years earlier, I had thought of sharing "my story," but just wasn't psychologically ready to let it out.

It was, in part, not wanting to let it be known that I had a "terminal illness," and felt as if I had in some ways, been leading a double life. And knowing that sharing this information about my health frankly changes the way some people look at you. Like so many others with cancer, you don't always want to explain to people the details of it, or complain about it, or want people to constantly "feel sorry" for you. At least, I didn't.

After I didn't get the Surgeon General gig in 2009, I began re-writing the notes and manuscripts that I'd developed earlier, but then there were still a lot of curve balls in my life that were coming my way, which put the book project on hold. Also, some of the "gut-wrenching stories" were hard to re-live.

It was only after my recent prostate cancer surgery that I felt in my heart it was time to let the story out—in hopes that it might inspire others to keep trying, don't quit, don't let labels that people place on you define who you are. Above all else— know that many of the obstacles that are thrown your way are really just "bumps" in the road, although they don't seem like it at the time, and that overcoming these obstacles will provide you with new strength, wisdom, and even a sense of happiness, knowing that you've made it.

Throughout my life's journey, the obstacles of being labeled "slow," severe colorblindness, and the "death sentence" of having "two years to live" didn't deter me from trying to find solutions to my obstacles, always trying to think "outside the box" in addition to exploring the "usual" solutions.

During the writing process, I rummaged through old boxes filled with hundreds of letters I'd kept from grateful patients, as well as awards and accolades—Surgeon of The Year, Humanitarian of the Year Award for operating on refugees, an American Cancer Society research grant, TV awards from the Associated Press, Outstanding Teacher of the Year Award from Purdue. From PhD psychologist, to Head & Neck Surgeon, to TV medical correspondent, and all the other careers that I've had—one principle holds true: You are not defined by your successes nor defeats, but whether you continue to try, thrive, and make a difference in other peoples' lives.

Hopefully, this book will inspire those who have faced obstacles to keep trying. As Thomas Alva Edison said: "Genius is 1% inspiration and 99% perspiration." Hard work is the backbone of success and genius. While many of the theories of why I took certain supplements and medications have (I believe) scientific merit, as a scientist, I know they still have to be tested properly. I hope that "my protocol" (or portions of it) will be explored in scientific trials—to possibly help people with MDS and other cancers. My experience is only one anecdotal case, but I'm certain these supplements and other medications I have taken kept me alive—against all odds. I'm grateful to have beaten the odds—it allowed me to write this book and share this knowledge.

Ultimately I feel blessed and fortunate that I've made it this far, and that I finished the book when I did. Timing is everything. As I begin my 65th orbit around the sun, approaching 15 years since my original MDS diagnosis, I've asked myself: "What's next?" Who knows what's next—learning not to just be alive, but to live. Stay tuned—still a work in progress.

AFTERWORD

by Steve Alexander

I walked onto the plane, just upgraded to First Class for the second leg of my trip from Denver to Pittsburgh, thankful that all my miles in the air paid off and I'd have the occasional luxury of the space to spread out and get my work done. Looking forward to time for preparing my client retreat, I thought to myself, "I hope I don't sit next to a 'Chatty Cathy' for this leg of the flight—I really need quality time to complete my work."

My seatmate had other plans. I could hear him from the flight attendants' area, before I'd even entered the cabin, on his mobile phone, talking about some television deal and thought, "Oh, no." What unfolded, however, was a "meeting" that changed both our lives—as those Universal experiences can do. If we're open to them. Mindful. Like a vessel described in many of the Zen parables I'd studied. Here comes the test, Steve. Ommmmmmm.

Paul Nemiroff turned out to be one of the most fascinating people I've ever met flying. Or anywhere for that matter. His inquisitiveness about who I was (he may have been looking over my shoulder as I was reading some medical document, compliments of the Medical Board of California, where I was serving as its president at the time, and his curiosity got the best of him), what I did, where I was going, and what I was doing there—was like a child who's seen the zoo animals for the first time.

He is an MD With a PhD in psychology. A practiced and accomplished professional. And yet a student of life. Curious. Genuine. Honest. Open. Caring. Interested and interesting. What I quickly realized was—here was a guy without pretense. Egoless. Driven, yet by his commitment to growing and becoming a fuller human being, not just human doing. In many conversations since, he's reached deeply into his soul to share his own struggles and challenges. And has heard mine. Without judgment or evaluation. Only with a deep desire to be helpful, a good listener, healer and nurturer. And a learner, too.

His life is an open book. Like this one. Talking about his list of credentials and accomplishments can be done by someone else.What I can tell you about Paul is he lives in his heart. His innate intelligence is obvious when you read about him. And what he's accomplished. What you can't know simply by reading is who he really is. And how tender and hopeful that heart is.

It's a universal truth—we all struggle. But it's what we become by and through those struggles that matters. I hope you've enjoyed this book as much as I have, and that it took you on a journey into the challenges he's overcome and how he's done it—into the person he's become and how he got there. What Paul has become is a man of heart. And soul. Of character and depth. His journey could shed light on yours. Maybe knock over an assumption or two. And carry you forward, gently.

That flight to Pittsburgh from Denver seemed to last only a

few minutes. By the time we ended, he and I both had a hunch there would be another conversation. Or two. Or more. There have been. And I've been the better person for it.

There's a lot more to say about Paul, and this book tells his story surely better than I could. I hope you enjoyed getting to know Paul. Let his words—his life—seep in slowly, like honey dripping into a teapot filled with a herbal tea brought to life by the subtle sweetness that's poured in and becomes one with the flavor, the very essence of the herb. That's what getting to know Paul has been like. And my own life's journey has been sweeter because of it.

———————————————

Steve Alexander has been appointed by three governors of the State of California as President of the Medical Board of California, Chairman of the California Board of Behavioral Sciences and a member of the State Athletic Commission. He has also served as director of the largest public relations firm in the world and now president of his own company, The Steve Alexander Group, where he coaches and trains doctors, Nobel Laureates, and executives on topics ranging from public speaking, to inspiring leadership, to creating new visions for companies.

APPENDIX

My Protocol

The essence of the supplements in this protocol are that they all have one or more of the following properties: anti-oxidant, anti-inflammatory, or anti-neoplastic (i.e. anti-cancer)—based on hundreds of research studies, albeit relatively few have been done on humans in controlled, double-blind, gold-standard fashion.

Two excellent references that address many of the specific supplements that I take and have detailed references to research articles on the mechanisms of action are:

1. *PDR for Nutritional Supplements,* 2nd Edition, 2008: Published by Physicians Desk Reference Inc. at Montvale, NJ 07645 by Sheldon Hendler, PhD, MD, FACP, FACN;

2. *PDR for Herbal Medicines,* 4th Edition, 2007 published by Thomson Healthcare Inc. at Montvale, NJ 07645, with forward by David Heber, MD, PhD, FACP,FACN Director, UCLA Center for Human Nutrition and UCLA botanical Research Center, UCLA School of Medicine.

Of course, there are literally hundreds of articles and research papers that go into great detail on each of the supplements, medications, and potential benefits of the substances listed below. Listing them all is beyond the scope of this book.

Many of the amounts of supplements I take go well beyond the minimum daily values discussed by the government.

Therefore, do not just casually take a bunch of supplements and "hope for the best." Supplements, just like medications or drugs, can have side effects and interact with other medications or foods. Again, always check with your health care professional before beginning any supplement program. Also, always discuss any medications you may be taking with your health care professional.

However, it's important to realize that minimum daily values are just that—minimum. In the case of Vitamin C, for example, the daily value set forth by the FDA for 100% is only 60 milligrams—that's to prevent Vitamin C deficiency-related diseases, such as scurvy, not to necessarily create "optimum health." I don't know too many Americans interested in only "average health"—and if given a choice, many might try to "optimize health." With respect again to just Vitamin C, at least 200 milligrams per day, or possibly much higher, may be useful to maximize the vitamin's potential health benefits, according to some scientists. [Frei, B., et al., (2012). *Authors' perspective: What is the optimum intake of Vitamin C in humans?* Critical Reviews in Food Science and Nutrition, Vol. 52, No. 9, pp. 815-829.]

Vitamin B Complex

One tablet, taken once a day, consisting of an assortment of various B vitamins (including thiamin 100 mg, riboflavin 20 mg, niacin 25mg, B6 2mg, folic acid 400 micrograms, B12 15 micrograms, Biotin, 30 micrograms, and pantothenic acid, 5.5 mg)

Vitamin B metabolizes carbohydrates, fats, amino acids and protein in the body. In other words, they play a role in breaking down food in the body and assisting with its conversion to energy. These vitamins are thought to play a key role for healthy nerve function as well, helping to maintain skin and eye health and **help produce red blood cells** in the body to assist with DNA synthesis and repair.* As mentioned, patients with MDS may have problems with red blood cell production.

Vitamin C

2000 mg per day (at least) in divided doses—9 a.m. and 9 p.m.

Vitamin C is an essential nutrient that supports immune system health and provides anti-oxidant support. It is also involved in collagen formation, which is important for healthy skin and connective tissue.*

Vitamin D3 (Cholecalciferol)

5,000-10,000 IUs per day depending on my blood levels.

Lower than normal levels of Vitamin D are becoming epidemic in the United States. The reasons are many and varied. Vitamin D acts like a hormone in the body and has many critical functions. Even when a person doesn't have any symptoms of say muscle weakness, or bone pain, you can still have a Vitamin D deficiency. Low blood levels of Vitamin D have been associated with:

- Increased risk of death from cardiovascular disease
- Cognitive impairment in older adults
- Severe asthma in children
- Cancer

Research suggests that Vitamin D could play a role in the prevention and treatment of a number of different conditions, including Type 1 and Type 2 diabetes, hypertension, glucose intolerance, and multiple sclerosis, as well as reducing one's risks of certain cancers. In Leukemia, 1997 11 (9): 1546-53 for example, Sokoloski reviewed several antioxidants in conjunction with Vitamin D and Vitamin E with a possible positive impact on MDS patients. Doctors disagree on an optimum number for Vitamin D levels in your body, but I shoot for at least 50ng/ml. Again, this is something that, like all of the supplements and protocol elements listed here, must be monitored closely by your physician or health care professional.*

DHEA

25 mg/day—thought to stimulate immune system.*

DHEA is a "parent hormone" produced by the adrenal glands near the kidneys and in the liver. In men, DHEA is also secreted by the testes. It is changed in the body to a hormone called androstenedione. Androstenedione is then changed into the major male and female hormones. DHEA levels seem to go down as we age. DHEA levels also seem to be lower in people with certain medical conditions. Some scientists believe that replacing DHEA with supplements might prevent some diseases and conditions.* An article written by Casson, P., 1992, American Journal of OB/GYN, revealed that physiologic supplementation of DHEA was associated with improvement in monocyte numbers (a type of white cell) and increased the number of "NK cells" or "killer t cells" that help fight infections in some patients—which can be the case with MDS.

Vitamin E

200-400 IUs per day

Vitamin E is an important vitamin required for the proper function of many organs in the body. It is also an antioxidant. It may help slow down processes that damage cells. Vitamin E has also been studied in preventing various cancers, including lung, oral, colorectal, pancreatic and prostate.* For example, an article in the British Journal of Hematology in 1997 by Peddie, 99 (3): 625-31, revealed evidence of oxidative damage from free radicals (those "bullies of the body" we talked about earlier) being more common in MDS patients, and that certain antioxidants may be of benefit.*

Coenzyme Q10

100-300 mg each day (varied over the years)

Coenzyme Q10 is involved with energy production within virtually nearly all cells in the human body. Its chemical name is Ubiquinone from the word "ubiquitous" meaning present everywhere. It has been shown to have benefit for those who take cholesterol lowering drugs [statins] as well as many other maladies.* Recent studies have even looked at it for possible benefits with certain subsets of those patients with MDS. For example, Dr. Azra Raza, who is a world authority on MDS and is a professor of medicine at Columbia University, has looked at coenzyme Q10 as well as ginger and curumin/tumeric as a potential treatment for certain MDS patients. As you will note below, I also take curcumin/tumeric. As we age, stress, poor diet and other factors can lower this critical substance in our body.

Omega 3 Fish Oils

3 grams a day —with essential DHA + EPA fish oils

Omega-3 fatty acids are polyunsaturated fatty acids that are essential nutrients for health. Numerous body functions depend on Omega-3-fatty acids, such as controlling blood clotting and supporting cell membranes in the brain. Our bodies cannot make omega-3 fats, so we must get them through food, or possibly supplements. Omega-3 fatty acids are being researched extensively and are thought by many scientists, to be helpful in heart disease and stroke. New studies are also identifying potential benefits for a wide range of conditions including certain cancers, inflammatory bowel disease, and rheumatoid arthritis.* Again, this ties into the anti-oxidant, and anti-inflammatory aspects of the protocol.

Resveratrol

100 mg per day

Resveratrol, a substance that exists in red wine and a natural plant compound, has antioxidant and inflammatory properties. Research shows that resveratrol may prevent blood clots and inhibit the growth of cancer cells; other studies suggest that it may have a positive impact on longevity.* *A Study in Blood,* 2003 102(3):987-95 by Estrov Z. et. al. showed that it had anti-leukemic activities, and as such one could speculate its potential positive impact on MDS.

Green Tea

100 mg per day

Green tea is known to assist healthy cells in virtually all stages of growth. There are some indications green tea may help destroy cancer cells. A major substance in green tea is something called "EGCG" and has been established as the compound responsible for Green tea's wide range of health benefits. Most of the studies on green tea have focused on the cancer protective aspects. The potent antioxidant compounds have demonstrated greater antioxidant protection than Vitamins C and E, in some experimental studies. With respect to green tea and cancer patients, one study by Suzuki, K. et. al in Anticancer Res, 2012 32(6): 2369-75, suggested that the antioxidant effect of green tea extract on reactive oxygen species (free radicals) produced by neutrophils (a type of white blood cell that fights bacterial infections) may be effective in reducing oxidative stress in cancer patients, meaning that those "bullies of the body" may not be able to "bully" normal cells as much.*

Also, new animal and clinical studies suggest that EGCG may play a role in prevention of cancer by suppressing tumor development by decreasing or inhibiting certain inflammatory agents in the body (e.g. something called "tumor necrosis factor alpha"). *[For more information on this, see the two main references listed at the start of the Appendix: Nutritional Supplements PDR and the Herbal Medicine PDR.]*

Alpha Lipoic Acid

400 mg per day

"ALA" is a vitamin-like antioxidant that helps fight cell damaging free radicals. Alpha lipoic acid is thought to work as an antioxidant in water and fatty tissue, which permits it to enter all parts of the nerve cell and protect it from damage theoretically. Some of the research on it has looked at its effect on diseases of aging as well as "peripheral neuropathy," a problem associated with symptoms that include pain, burning, numbness, tingling and weakness and that can be caused by injury, nutritional deficiencies, chemotherapy and others.*

Melatonin

3 mg at night (extended release)

The hormone melatonin is thought to produce a number of health benefits in terms of your immune system. It's a powerful antioxidant and free radical scavenger that is thought to fight inflammation. It's also involved in regulating your sleep-wake cycle, and is produced by a gland in our brain, the pineal gland. As we age, the amount of melatonin we generate decreases. Besides the sleep aid effect that most people have heard of, melatonin also has potential anti-cancer benefits.*

Research on melatonin has shown that it inhibits the proliferation of a wide range of cancer cell types, as well as triggering cancer cell apoptosis (self destruction). The hormone also can interfere with the new blood supply tumors require for their rapid growth (angiogenesis). Melatonin may also decrease the toxicity of cancer chemotherapy. Other studies suggest that melatonin reduced the growth of prostate cancer. Similarly encouraging results for lung, pancreatic, colorectal and other types of cancer, as well as improving survival rates in certain situations, have also been suggested.*

Coconut Oil

2000 mg per day

Coconut oil is thought to have many potential health benefits. With respect to the immune system, it is thought to possibly strengthen it because it contains antimicrobial lipids or "fats," which have antifungal, antibacterial and antiviral properties.*

Turmeric / Curcumin Complex

400 mg per day (at least)

These agents are thought to have anti-inflammatory and possible anti-neoplastic properties as well.* Diets containing garlic, onion, soy, turmeric, ginger, tomatoes, green tea and chilies that are common in Asia are associated with a lower risk of a variety of cancers ranging from colon, GI tract, breast, leukemias and lymphomas. Some of these dietary agents and their biologic activities have now been studied as potential preventive agents for cancer. Turmeric belongs to the ginger family and curcumin is its most active component. Turmeric and curcumin have been found to have a variety of mechanisms of action according to some researchers, including:*

- inhibiting or suppressing certain inflammatory chemicals in the body (e.g. something called Anti-TNF and anti-TGFb)

- inhibiting new blood vessel growth to tumors (Anti-angiogenic)

- inhibiting or reducing certain enzyme reactions that could speed up the cancer

- inhibiting cancer cells from growing faster (Anti-proliferative effects)

- improving the body's response to certain chemotherapy or radiation treatments (Sensitization of cells to chemo and radiation therapies)

In lay terms, this simply means that there appear to be anti-oxidant, anti-inflammatory and anti-cancer properties in these substances.*

Probiotics and Digestive Enzymes

Within the last five years I have added these to "my protocol." There is research to show that both of these supplements can support the immune system through a variety of mechanisms.

* To be clear, all of the above are considered "supplements" by the FDA, and don't require a prescription. As such, there is a standard disclaimer for virtually all supplements that reads something like this: "These statements have not been evaluated by the Food and Drug Administration. Supplements as defined by the FDA are not intended to diagnose, treat, cure or prevent any disease."

*   *   *

The substances below are considered "drugs" or medications and have specific indications and regulations, and require a prescription, but can be prescribed sometimes "off label," meaning that research and/or the doctor have suggested other than the "standard" uses for various problems may be appropriate.

HGH—Human Growth Hormone

Somatropin (rDNA origin) prefilled pens. Dosage will vary considerably depending on what your doctor says and believes.

Probably the most controversial substance of my regimen is Human Growth Hormone, or HGH. There is a lot of negative press about how it has been abused in sports and other areas. Some people are using it at many hundreds of times the recommended dosage, not to save their life, but to enhance their sports performance or perhaps they think it will make themselves appear more youthful. I use a physiologic dose that puts me in a "normal" range for a person about 40 years old.

My use of HGH was only based on a theoretic premise that it could help my immune system and possibly help me with my blood cancer. After reviewing 100s of articles about its possible beneficial effects, including the positive impact or stimulation of certain killer T cells, it made sense. However, there were still some concerns (including from some oncologists) that it could actually make things worse. With this in mind, it was made sure that my approximate blood levels of this substance were carefully monitored and never became above a safe threshold.

Every morning I give myself injections of HGH to create something called "physiologic levels." The goal is not to dial back the clock, but rather to keep me alive through promoting a vital, strong immune system.

Testosterone Injections

Exact amount will vary considerably. I use intramuscular injections twice a week to keep my levels in the 500-600 NG/DL (Nanograms per Decilter) range. A normal range for testosterone varies considerably among doctors/labs and of course your age.

I use limited testosterone injections—again to maintain healthy levels—which is thought by many researchers (although not all, certainly) to play a positive role in your immune system. The testosterone, in turn, can also indirectly help my red blood cell count. In fact, years ago testosterone supplementation was used with cancer patients to help them to boost their red blood cell count. Interestingly, this part of the treatment is something "old" that has become something "new" again. It should be reemphasized that I am carefully monitored by physicians for any side effects—*"Don't try this at home."*

There are thousands of articles on these topics, which is beyond the scope or intention of this book. I suggest, for those interested, to check out first, some of the "lay articles" on line, as well as the references mentioned above, and then dig deeper by going to pub med perhaps to see some of the latest actual scientific research.

I advise you to have a medical dictionary available as you go through the articles that have "medical speak" in them. The best advice (in my opinion) is to actually talk with a physician who is knowledgeable about complimentary medicine / integrative medicine and allopathic medicine, and who has experience in both—i.e. "trained traditionally," but continued learning, studying and researching about alternative approaches that may have benefits.

Of course, the MDS (Myelodysplastic) Foundation is a fantastic organization and resource for those with this disease, as well as the American Cancer Society. It should be noted that, by my mentioning of these organizations, it is not intended or suggested that they in any way necessarily endorse, approve, or recommend my protocol. That is something I decided to do on my own, of course with careful monitoring by my physicians.

Also, I took antibiotics when I had a bacterial infection, which I'm still prone to get more frequently than the average person. And sometimes, I also use Neupogen® that stimulates my body to produce more white blood cells. In other words, I wasn't throwing away more traditional treatments only for experimental ones, but borrowing from both.

The goal of my protocol was to enhance the immune system and decrease the free radical load, as well as reducing excessive inflammation in my body. As simplistic as it sounds, I truly believe this protocol has something to do with extending my life. At the time of my initial diagnosis, my median survival was just two years. No therapy for MDS, at the time, was shown to actually prolong survival. At the time of this writing, it's about **15 years** since my diagnosis. No one expected me to live this long.

As a scientist, I realize that controlled studies need to be performed. I hope this book is a catalyst to encourage pilot studies on new alternative treatments for MDS and other cancers in the quest for a cure.

ACKNOWLEDGEMENTS

To the Myelodysplastic (MDS) Foundation—for all the incredible work and tireless hours you all put into educating people about this vicious disease and giving people hope about new treatments for the future.

Thank you Dr. John Bennett for the support you've been for me all these years.

Dr. Dale Rice and Dr. Paul Ward, who at UCLA were true doctors—in the Latin sense of the word: "teacher." There were many others, but they have stood out in my mind as truly great teachers.

Dr. Don King, my major advisor at Purdue University while working on my PhD, provided strong and deliberate guidance, to make me the best I could be.

To Steve Alexander our "chance" meeting was clearly not by chance. You have been an inspiration with your insights and wisdom about life. Thank you!

To all my doctors/oncologists/hematologists and others, and especially my oncologist Dr. Richard Gualtieri, who supported me in the way I hope all patients get supported during the best and worst of times. Rich provided me with technical information, was always available, but most importantly was compassionate and could "talk me off the wire" when I thought I would be "checking out" soon.

To Dr. Mukherjee, author of *The Emperor of All Maladies: A Biography of Cancer*—your words and history of cancer provided tremendous inspiration to me while writing my book and battling MDS as well as prostate cancer. I have given your book to numerous doctors in the hopes that this "plague of our generation," as you mention, will be overcome. Thank you for continuing to "fight the good fight."

To Dr. James Garlington—mentor, friend and wonderful human being.

To Dr. Dexter Blome—Dex, what can I say, we've been through the "wars" together.

To Dr. Tom Ollerman—"OLLY"—"But that's OK"—as good as you are, some patients can't always be "fixed."

To Charlie Amidon—thanks buddy for always watching my back.

To Dr. Michael Spitzer—you've been there for me for a long time—thank you. Your real title should be Mayor of Orange County, or at least Newport.

To a fellow Sigma Chi, Brother John Waskom, thank you for being there for me as a "Nemiroff interloper" all these years. Your guidance and counsel have been priceless.

To Mike Segars—thanks for all your availability, expertise, and for keeping us both out of the "big house."

Thank you to Arnold Mann for helping me get some of my ideas down on paper and being a caring human being.

To Steve Gross—thank you for the support, wisdom and especially making those long drives out to Palm Springs—even when it was 110 degrees.

To Tommy "I know a guy" Penna—your friendship has helped me through some hard times…thank you.

To the team at Sarati who help me produce Joint Formula 88®—including Barbara Creighton, Melody Bockelman, Hamilton Musser, Rebecca Campos, and the amazing staff—thank you for making Joint Formula 88 a huge success.

To Dan Hughes—a phenomenal QVC host and friend. Your calming influence helped me so much with my "pre-air jitters." I promise not to bring out the "model knee" anymore.

To the 1000s of patients over the years who allowed me the privilege of being their physician and surgeon—I hope I helped make a positive difference and followed medicine's foundational rule—"First do no harm."

To all the new, young physicians—I hope you find mentors who teach you the true meaning of the patient-doctor relationship, as opposed to the relationship between "consumer" and "provider." I look forward to intelligent tort reform that is truly just to all parties involved. Some insurance carriers have stepped up to the plate with innovative solutions, that also garnered a reasonable profit—I hope they will join with others including top physicians to address the issues of high quality and affordable medicine, making the USA once again number one in the world.

To the "kids"—Nicole, Rachael, Guy, and Lauren—with love. May you fulfill your dreams and remember to "give back."

To Maritza Wilson, my Godchild—I'm so thrilled we have reconnected. You are also a joy in my life.

To my brother Art, and sister-in-law Ute—thanks for being there—always.

I would greatly like to thank Brian Solon for his editing skills, his persistence, and most importantly helping me stay on track while I reminisced through the 100s of stories in my life. Without his skill, I couldn't have finished the book. Brian, timing is everything. Thank you Brian!

To my wife Patrice with love and gratitude. She is someone who's helped keep me alive all these years with love, hope and inspiration—another day of "bliss" darlin'—"Everyday's a party."

Paul Nemiroff, PhD, MD, FACS is a nationally recognized surgeon who received his MD from UCLA and holds a PhD from Purdue University. He has published and presented hundreds of articles and research papers on surgical techniques, hyperbaric oxygen, and complementary medical therapies. He has performed over 10,000 surgeries, and scored highest in the country on the Head & Neck Surgery Exams (99%). He's an award-winning TV medical correspondent and recipient of over a dozen national awards including one from the American Cancer Society. Dr. Nemiroff was invited to the White House and considered a candidate for Surgeon General of the United States.

Brian Solon is a writer and editor whose works include *In Pursuit, Think Big Act Small, Ignited, Love At First Cut, Illegal Beings,* and *The Road To Reality.* He grew up in Northern California, studied music at UC Berkeley, and produced the global launch of *Star Trek* with director JJ Abrams and Paramount Pictures. He has a JD from Santa Clara University, an MBA from Haas Business School, and lives in New York.